THE ORIGIN AND EVOLUTION OF HUMAN VALUES

CLIFFORD SHARP

THE ORIGIN AND EVOLUTION OF HUMAN VALUES

CLIFFORD SHARP

Pen Press
London

© Clifford Sharp 1997

All rights reserved.

First published in Great Britain by
Pen Press
Church House
Portland Avenue
Stamford Hill
London N16 6HJ

ISBN 1 900796 15 5

A catalogue record of this book is available
from the British Library.

Mandelbrot by Pericles 'Asher' Rospiglios
Cover design by Catrina Sherlock, Waves Graphics

Contents

Acknowledgments
Preface   I

Chapter 1 - An Introduction   1
Chapter 2 - Nature & Nurture   19
Chapter 3 - Biological & Genetic Origins   53
Chapter 4 - Schooling & Education   94
Chapter 5 - Ethics, Philosophies, Religions & Values   113
Chapter 6 - Behaviourism & Body Language   129
Finale   139
Appendix A   159
Appendix B   180

Index
Bibliography

ACKNOWLEDGMENTS

In a subject such as this, it is impossible to recognise, and adequately to acknowledge, my indebtedness to the many people who have influenced my thinking in this complex area. Undoubtedly my deepening interest started when working in India during the war years, and was stimulated by my talks with my Indian colleagues which caused me to question the somewhat simplistic views I had when I first went there. They made me realise that their very different values had a meaning and significance in their cultures which made me recognise mine were not necessarily 'right' for all people at all times and in all circumstances. I cannot today recall them all by name but would like to single out Mr Chatterjii, a Hindu of the Brahmin caste, who made me understand that wisdom was by no means the prerogative of Western culture and philosophy.

After I returned to London, late in 1946, at Redington's invitation I joined the Woolgatherer's Club, a group of actuaries who were concerned with the rapidly changing ethos of British Society. This resulted in a series of wide ranging discussions with Redington, Perks, Beard and others, many of those talks having a philosophical or ethical background. Rather to my surprise I found that my new views on the relative and cultural nature of values did not seem to command a ready acceptance.

Then for the next fifteen years I was too busy to be able to address the many questions which the subject throws up as soon as it is considered seriously but, all the time at the back of my mind, I had that unanswered question from my six year old great-nephew, "What is it all for?" which today, after years of reading and study, I still find unanswerable.

Obviously on a subject such as this, one is inevitably indebted to the hundreds of other authors one has read and, wherever it seemed appropriate, I have deliberately quoted extracts from those who most influenced my thinking, rather than attempting to paraphrase wordings which stated, succinctly, concepts which I believed to be true and which I therefore wanted to communicate and endorse. I would also like to mention the widening circle of writers I have now contacted via the Web. This has been made possible by Asher (Pericles 'Asher' Rospigliosi) whose timely assistance and advice has been a critical factor in this most welcome development. He has also provided the Mandelbrot picture for the cover which symbolises, for me, the complexity of the widespread ramifications of this vital subject.

Once I started writing I needed someone to test my growing convictions on, and Harold Purchase provided the touchstone I wanted. I do not think I have succeeded in persuading him wholly to my way of thinking but our correspondence certainly cleared my mind, making me re-write some parts of the now growing 'manuscript' time and again.

At various stages, what I have written has been shown to others, in particular to our son Lindsay whose penetrating comments played an important part in the shape of the final version, and I would also like to thank Peter and Shirley Turnbull for the time and effort they spent not only in vetting the material but also in questioning those places where my meaning was not clear to them. This process was continued by my editor Gloria Morrison who has played a major part in bringing the book out.

There is one general acknowledgment I would like to make and that is to the many people who have been responsible for transforming the computer into an effective tool, particularly for word processing. A book of this character would have been an impossible task for anyone like myself even to contemplate without the immense power which the desktop publisher has made so readily available.

Finally, my most important acknowledgment is to my wife Olive for her understanding and tolerance for the many, many hours I have sat in front of this keyboard and screen!

Clifford Sharp
Gillingham, Dorset
1996

The Origin and Evolution of Human Values

"What is it all for?"

*"And the Lord God formed man of the dust of the ground, and breathed into his nostrils the breath of life, **AND MAN BECAME A LIVING SOUL.**" Genesis 2:7*

As life evolved something strange happened - 'values' emerged. To us this change, this jump in the way the world and the Universe was perceived, came with the emergence of humanity as we now know it when, in Biblical terms 'man became a living soul'. Since then humanity has been faced with that so far unanswered (and probably unanswerable) question *'What **IS** it all for?'*

Religions and cultures have each provided their particular mythical answer (I use 'myth' in its strict sense of something held to be true by faith not reason) and have then translated that answer into a code of ethics (we call 'values'). From our own culture each of us has developed our unique and personal 'values' which we use to assess our own 'interests' and what we assess to be the 'interests' and 'values' of others. This strongly influences our behaviour.

The main, pragmatic, purpose of philosophy, of ethics, of much of religious teaching, (and of any ethical morality derived from studies of such subjects) must surely be to modify patterns of human behaviour in appropriate ways. Ways which it is considered should help the members of a society to live together more easily, to behave in a more 'seemly' fashion; thus interacting more readily by eliminating, as far as is practicable, the conflicts which lead to the malicious actions covered so well in the telling phrase - 'Man's inhumanity to Man' - the dangerous feature of human behaviour characterizing so much of human history. Something which, in the twentieth century, has falsified the rational beliefs of the eighteenth and the easy optimism of the nineteenth.

• The Fundamental Questions

What are 'values'? What is 'right' and what is 'wrong'? How important are they? And where do they come from?

The first question is, in many ways, the most difficult to answer since we use the word 'values' in such different ways. There seems to be three broad classes of 'values' - first the type which relate to the individual such as 'good' and 'bad' which, when considered carefully, can be related primarily to the person - 'good' or 'bad' for whom? The second are 'values' where there is, normally, an element of consensus implied in the terms such as 'fair', 'decent', 'seemly' and 'tolerant' while the third uses value judgment in a quite different way relating primarily to things in the sense of 'fitting', that is to say appropriate for purpose, such as a 'good' pen, a 'good' computer, a 'good' tennis racquet. I am not concerned with this third class.

With regard to the first two there are two separate and important aspects - first, how does each culture establish its current commonly accepted 'values'? And second, how does each individual acquire the unique 'values' which are specific for him, or for her, given that all such individual 'values' must, inevitably, be strongly coloured, and, indeed, be broadly determined, by the culture in which each individual was born, bred and matured?

At this stage I must emphasize there are two other issues which need to be clearly differentiated; first what 'values' are (and how they are acquired) and second what those 'values' should be. This, clearly, is in itself a 'value' judgment. My principle objective is to deal with the first aspect, to clarify what human 'values' are, how we acquire them and what their overwhelming importance is in all aspects of life. Later I suggest a partial and generalized answer to the second.

- **What is meant by 'Values'**

For my purpose the word covers the concepts involved in the words 'good' and 'bad', 'right' and 'wrong', 'tolerant' and 'intolerant', 'loving' and 'hateful', (and particularly I suggest, 'fair' and 'unfair', 'decent' and its opposite) applied specifically to behaviour. Such 'values' provide each of us with the unique personal moral template we use (mostly subconsciously) to assess and then usually to judge the intentions and actions of others (and of ourselves). Also to assess the importance to us of the likely outcome of the interaction of those various actions and reactions. As will be developed later many of our 'values' are derived from the myths about ourselves, our culture and our place in the universe (our personal cosmology) which provide the largely unconscious framework within which we live and have our being. They are the pragmatic outcome of the answers we have adopted as true (mostly without much critical consideration) to the fundamental questions posed by philosophy, ethics and religion. And for most of us that personal cosmology derives far more from intuition and faith rather than from logic!

While we all have to take the purpose of our very existence 'on trust' this does not matter provided the 'values' we acquire, and live by, result in actions which are socially desirable, those generally regarded as 'fair', 'decent' and 'seemly' according to the culture in which we live. If by choice, or by force of circumstance, we move into a materially different culture (or if perhaps we acquire a mate with 'values' very different from our own?) then there can be a 'culture shock' which can cause problems for both ourselves and others.

- **How important are 'values'?**

Accepting then the objective, in pragmatic terms, of most of philosophy, ethics and much of religion must be to establish patterns of behaviour of a socially acceptable kind this must be effected by influencing the 'values' of individuals. The developing current debate on how socially acceptable (and socially efficient) 'values' can be induced (particularly through the framework of an educational system) is growing in intensity. It would therefore seem that a sound understanding of how 'Values' originate and evolve is likely to be vital in encouraging those changes which are considered to be socially necessary.

The basic facts are that, on this planet (minuscule and insignificant as it is in terms of the Universe) conscious life has evolved. Why, we do not know but each culture, each religion, has developed its own myths to provide some kind of answer, some framework, for the ordinary individual to use (without too much effort) enabling us to develop a conceptual structure within which to survive, to enjoy life to the full as far as we can and, for most, to pass on what we regard as the more important of those 'values', to a younger generation.

- **The Scientific Method & our Mastery over our Environment**

The dramatic, and it seems, irreversible increase in the numbers of our species (with its massive impact on other species, on the atmosphere and on the rest of our terrestrial environment) clearly call for a new type of adaptation derived from new perceptions and, therefore, new 'values'. Otherwise our overwhelming success in manipulating our physical environment (and probably our genetic characteristics) may well condemn us to a relatively `early` partial or full extinction.

As one leading American anthropologist has written:-

'What we need today is a way of thinking, something deliberately dreamed up in the twentieth century and learned by all members of our species, to protect the lives of future generations and preserve their options.'

Surely this must involve a fundamental change in many of humanity's 'values' and it is therefore vital we should understand just how those values originate and evolve. As a species we have survived from a very unpromising start through our ability to adapt and, now circumstances have changed dramatically and there seem to be few really safe havens, it is urgent we should show that mental resourcefulness once again in perhaps a very different form.

• **Humanity's Early Days**

In the earliest days of Homo sapiens there was a centrifugal force which caused mankind to spread, slowly, over the earth originating highly resourceful ways of coping with the extreme variations in climate and environment it encountered. This led to forms of specialization varying from the Bushmen of the Kalahari and the Aborigines of Australia, to the Eskimos in the arctic regions of Northern Canada. This widespread distribution, and the isolation that inevitably went with it, led to an amazing diversity of cultures and of individual 'values' which, while they show some common basic biological basis, varied widely in all other respects. These 'values', and the patterns of behaviour which went with them, changed, usually very slowly, over the millennia sometimes involving cultures, such as the Egyptian, which survived for many generations, sometimes causing others, like the Olmec in South America, to disappear almost without trace after an historically short time.

Like all other forms of life, particularly mobile life, humanity is a problem solving organism. To deal with the difficulties stemming from such varied environments, humanity developed first a complex of spoken languages and then later, much later, when a certain degree of civilization had been achieved, various forms of written languages. These two factors greatly improved our ability to communicate, and thus to spread knowledge of the best solution to the immediate problems, so that the Iron Age slowly followed the Bronze Age which itself had overtaken the Stone Age.

Later, comparatively recently, came printing and now the electronic transfer of information both of which dramatically improved communications and, therefore, humanity's overall problem solving and communication capacities. These have increased still further our mastery over our environment. The recent developments, while undoubtedly adding to our power, have not necessarily resulted in the longer-term happiness of humanity.

- **Early Family Groups**

Initially humanity's spread would have been in relatively small family groups and for these to reproduce, and to multiply, reasonably acceptable forms of behaviour had to be developed and transmitted from one generation to another. This meant that the appropriate 'values' controlling behaviour had to be evolved. Later, as the groups increased in size, and individuals started to specialize, the factors of integration and interdependence, became paramount and individuals had to learn to accept more fully the idea that responsibility to the group sometimes overrode their personal self-interest. This is a 'value' which, to a material extent, seems to be in jeopardy in some parts of the West today.

For many millennia the 'values' suitable for the family unit and the tribe were all that mattered and then (it seems somewhere about ten thousand years ago) came the earliest civilizations of which we have any real evidence. These supported more detailed specialization which led to the written recording of knowledge involving more complex and more sophisticated sets of 'values', thus encouraging and facilitating the more complex interactions enabling the group, and the culture, to be maintained against the challenges, both natural and human, they faced.

• Ancient Egyptian 'Values

Any realistic analysis of the origin of social 'values' is far beyond my scope but it is worth recording that the earliest statement I have so far found comes from about BC 2000 where (anticipating much of the Judaic/Christian rules spelt out by Moses) the Ancient Egyptian 'Book of the Dead' pictures the god Osiris as testing the newly dead to decide whether his, or her, soul was fit to be allowed to live with him (Osiris) in the hereafter.

The form of the protestations recorded in the tombs provides an insight into the approved 'values'. They have a surprisingly familiar ring consisting of statements that the individual had not stolen, been covetous, killed a human, told lies, committed adultery or abused a young boy which would provide most of the basic mores needed for a civilized society to prosper even today. It will be appreciated that from an early stage in the development of Ancient Egyptian mythology the concept of a personal life after death held a central place and this was inevitably passed on to many of the succeeding religions including the Judaic/Christian/Muslim.

• The Position Today

According to current scientific thinking in the West we are beginning to make, we believe, intelligent guesses at 'When' and even, possibly, 'How' the Universe started but no one has yet provided any kind of final, convincing and reasoned, answer to the 'Why?' In the foreseeable future this is likely to remain an enigma for most thinking people. Since we are unlikely to find any rational answer to that basic question we must make some assumption (either consciously or not) on why we are here and, therefore, how we should behave.

To do this we can base ourselves on the myths we have been taught to accept as 'true' or, alternatively nowadays for many of us, just rely on blind faith holding that, somewhere, there is a 'meaning' and that the whole incredible complexity and beauty (in our eyes) of the Universe is not, as someone once said just 'A cosmic jest'.

Today the intensity, and multiplicity, of the interaction of 'values' which we face, demand we strive to establish, world-wide, a solid basis for tolerance since otherwise, our particular culture must, it seems more than likely, lead to some form of racial suicide on a global scale. The study of the origin, and evolution, of our own 'values' and the need to understand more fully the importance of their interaction with others are therefore of vital concern to us all.

- **'Values' are more 'Caught' than 'Taught'**

Although I cannot cite any scientific evidence to support this thesis, I suggest genetic inheritance makes each individual more, or less, susceptible to particular patterns of 'values' than to others. It seems possible that in this aspect of humanity, as in so many others, something like the 'normal distribution curve' may well apply so that while the majority of us (who lie somewhere in the middle of the distribution) have little or no trouble in taking up the ordinary 'values' which our native culture regards as 'right', there will always be a fringe element which, at one end of the distribution, will produce those we regard as 'saints' and at the other end the psychotics, the mass murderers, the rapists and the paedophiles who are ranked, by ordinary people, as 'evil'.

If this concept is soundly based (and it seems to be supported at least in part by the condition known as Asperger's disease where the sufferers have no idea of time so that they cannot appreciate the results of their actions) it may provide an answer to the problem of the existence of what most of us regard as 'evil' for surely abstract 'evil', as such, does not exist. However there certainly are people who, whether as children or adults, cannot be induced, or persuaded, to behave according to the basic rules society needs if civilized life is to continue reasonably smoothly.

• The Scientific Method and Environmental Control

Mankind's primary objective was, until early this century to master our terrestrial environment in order to survive and multiply. Now with the work in atomic physics associated with the development of Intercontinental Ballistic Missiles delivery systems on one hand, and the elimination of the greater part of the major population killer diseases on the other, we are facing challenges and problems for which, as a genus, we seem to be almost wholly unprepared. We are going to need all of our vaunted problem-solving ability to deal with challenges of this magnitude which, for their solution, depend not primarily on physical solutions, but on shifts in mental attitudes, in 'values', such as we have not seen hitherto.

In the Western world (and to a material extent in other cultures as well) educational systems are today heavily weighted in favour of the skills we believe we need to enhance our environmental mastery while the intellectual concepts (vital I hold to ensure the survival of our kind and our culture) are the ones most often given second place.

- **The Dramatic Changes in the last Century and a Half.**

During the last one hundred and fifty years there have been four new major 'discoveries', four new concepts, which have profoundly changed the way most Western men and women view themselves in relation to their cosmology. These were Darwin's proposal of evolution as the prime cause of the origin of species which shifted mankind from being regarded as the prima persona in the Universe so that we recognize we are but a part (for us an all-important part) of the sequence of life on this planet. We are still working through many of the deeper implications of the evolutionary story he first widely publicized.

The second came from Einstein's concept of Relativity which, in the scientific sphere, undermined and finally superseded most if not all of the 'Absolutes' of the Newtonian cosmology. This revolutionary concept spread, slowly, to other areas of thought so that the implication that everything is relative became more acceptable - and that as Shakespeare makes Hamlet say *'There is nothing either good or bad but thinking makes it so.'*

The third stemmed from Freud's analysis of the way our minds operate with all that involved for education and finally the 'discovery' in quantum physics of the 'uncertainty principle' as a fundamental fact of the Universe as we now comprehend it, a principle which is now being associated, in the larger world, with the new theory of 'chaos'. The full implications of these are still to be realized in contemporary thought and it is far from clear what effect they are likely to have on currently acceptable values. Certainly they all lead us to question the certainties which our earlier culture took for granted.

• Character & Temperament

The relative importance of temperament, character and emotions and their influence on 'values', varies from one person to another differing with their sex and their circumstances; particularly how their interests and priorities are perceived, and assessed via the inevitably biased glass of their individual 'values'.

• The Pragmatic Approach

May I now I appeal to William James, the American philosopher, and to what he described as his pragmatic approach to philosophy when he asked:-

Do these concepts help to establish rules which enable each of us to decide what actions we ought to take and, with a somewhat different emphasis, should take?

There are two sayings which illustrate the point - the first is - *'As the twig is bent so grows the tree',* the second *'You can't make an oak out of an ash'* and finally there is the comment of an experienced headmaster who said *'No, but our job is to ensure the burgeoning tree becomes a 'good' oak or a 'good' ash'.* Now 'good' is obviously a 'value' judgement which has to be assessed according to someone's 'values' and the basic question then becomes 'good' for whom? Or for what? And 'according to whose 'values'? Which leads naturally to a search for Absolutes.

• Absolutes

In the Western World, starting certainly with the Greeks (and probably earlier in the East with the Hindus and the Buddhists), all the main prophets, wise men (and women) and philosophers have sought to establish 'Absolutes' which they considered must hold good for all humanity, at all times and in all circumstances but they have failed to find them. While such an approach may provide a useful discipline in considering the basic questions involved in seeking the origin of `values`, experience makes it clear that any formal statement of such 'Absolutes' has to be drawn in such wide terms as to provide only very general and limited guidance. Such statements lose their effectiveness when called upon to determine the 'right' action in widely differing circumstances. Simplistically `Good' is to be preferred to 'Bad', 'Benevolence' to 'Malevolence', 'Right' to 'Wrong' but just what these terms mean in each individual case, can only be determined, in the last resort, by our own 'values'.

• A Definition of Absolutes

Here it is useful to provide a definition of what I mean by Absolutes which some writers (such as the humanist Schiller) have referred to as 'the universals'. The most useful definition I have so far found is that given by Isaiah Berlin who referred to 'over-arching principles' going on to say he had failed to find them and that, in his opinion:- *'human values (moral, political, aesthetic and religious) have validity only within particular 'forms of life'* (i.e. traditions, cultures and societies).

• The Judaic Ten Commandments

As a simple example of an attempt to define a set of Absolute 'values' controlling human behaviour consider the Ten Commandments which provided the framework of much of early Judaic and later of Christian Law and which were, it seems, derived from concepts established in Egypt many centuries earlier.

In today's world, and with humanity's power over ourselves and our environment, they need elaborating, interpreting and extending since we have to deal with ethical problems of an entirely different order from those which the Jews then faced. The Commandments were a short and straightforward guide evolved for a Jewish society in its pastoral and migratory stage so that, for many centuries, they have needed sophisticated 'interpretations' to fit changing conditions.

In a similar fashion the American Constitution which, in the nineteenth century Gladstone described as one of the outstanding achievements of the human mind, has needed continuous revision and adjustment by decisions ('interpretations') of the Supreme Court to keep it reasonably in line with the changing culture and mores of contemporary life in the USA.

To cope, therefore, with today's immense increase in our control over the environment, needs, self evidently I believe, a much fuller understanding of how human 'values' originate and change.

- **The Place of Philosophy, Ethics & Religion**

Any investigation of this type must be regarded as 'philosophical' in its nature and so I was comforted by what William James stressed when he wrote that :- *'philosophy should be regarded more as expressing a general view of the world rather than as an exercise in seeking the correct solution*

to a particular set of philosophical problems.'
He also made the valid point that, in the long run, the acid test must be whether the ideas put forward on such subjects are acceptable to the broad mass of thinking people for such vitally important issues *"should not be regarded as solely the province of 'professional' philosophers."*

Seeking guidance in any attempt to define 'Absolutes' (universals) is what most, if not all, of our philosophies, ethical and religious studies are primarily about and some of the approaches and provisional answers are considered more fully in the Chapter on ' Ethics, Philosophies & Religions; The Search for Absolutes.'

If, then, we are willing to accept we do not know, and are not likely to know, the purpose of the Universe, *(What is it all for?* as the small boy most pertinently asked), we must work on the assumption there is some meaning so that the whole thing is not 'a cosmic jest', accepting life as we find it and making up our minds to enjoy our experience of it to the full, living with zest, aiming to see that our form of life (our particular culture and our personal 'values') will continue by passing them on to the next generation either directly to our children or, in their absence, to other people's.

Such 'values' should help us to 'force the djinni back into the bottle', the djinni our comparatively recently acquired powers derived from the scientific method have let loose on an almost wholly unprepared world. We now have controls and powers for which, in terms of the evolution of the human species, the very recent development of 'civilization' has not prepared us leaving mankind isolated and on the edge of a potential abyss with remarkably little guidance to help us.

May I make quite clear what my book is attempting is only a first step. To provoke discussion generally (and in the educational world too I hope) where, at the moment, it would seem all too much attention is being paid to the 'sciences' and all too little to the 'humanities'. I certainly do not pretend to provide all the answers but hope to move the discussion in a direction which, I believe, will, literally, be vital probably for our children and almost certainly for our children's' children.

• Summing Up

To enjoy life to the full we need 'values' which will encourage that zest for living as children, adolescents, adults and parents that will enable us to live a full life that will continue into what the French so aptly call 'le troisieme age'. Such values need to be staunch enough to sustain us in times of trial yet flexible enough to adjust as our body and mind change with age and experience. A tall order indeed!

I write then about 'values', how they have arisen, the part they play in determining actions, how we acquire them, how they change as we age and gain experience, how unique they are for each and every one of us, how we indicate them to others both consciously and unconsciously and, finally, the way in which we assess others' 'values' and 'interests' and how we then interact with them.

Any attempt to deal, fully, with such an incredibly complex subject would, I know, be an impossible undertaking (certainly in my lifetime) so that all I can do is to put forward an outline, to suggest ideas and approaches derived from my reading and influenced (strongly in some cases) by the people I have known in many parts of the world over the last eighty or more years.

I put this forward as 'a chopping block', something out of which a better version can, I believe, be moulded and crafted.

There must be a call for tolerance (common to the Christian and all the main world religions) which must be regarded as a fundamental to our future, but that even this 'virtue' has to be constrained by communal laws and mores restricting the actions arising from the antisocial 'values' of the small minority of deviants the mass murderers, paedophiles and other 'evil' personalities.

My approach should be regarded as a survey, an overall view, of the many aspects of what is involved in acquiring 'values', of 'coming to terms with life' and I hope what I have written will have a special appeal for those who have matured sufficiently to be conscious that their formal education has not provided them with the ideas and concepts they need to face many of the fundamental issues of life. Issues on which, consciously or unconsciously, they are going to have 'to take a view'.

It aims at providing a mental framework, a scale of reference, which will, I believe, help people to absorb realistic concepts and 'values' thus developing their character by establishing constructive lifetime objectives so that, in mid-life, they will not suddenly realize their initial objectives have become stultifying and unsatisfactory, forcing them to redirect their efforts in a major way.

As has been said very well *'there can be no real satisfaction in climbing to the top of the ladder only to find it is propped against the wrong wall'*.

I recognize it is highly unlikely that anyone else will agree with all I have written. However if it encourages, or provokes, another writer to deal more realistically, and constructively, with these important issues it will have more than served its purpose.

To end, as I began, with a quotation. Bernard Shaw wrote;- *'The reasonable man adapts himself to the world: the unreasonable one persists in trying to adapt the world to himself. Therefore all progress depends upon the unreasonable man.'*

but he failed to define what 'reasonable' was nor did he say what 'progress' was, the type of failure which unfortunately is all too common today. It so clearly depends on what 'values' are chosen as the 'right' yardstick!

Chapter 1

An Introduction

- *'There is nothing either good or bad but thinking makes it so' - Hamlet*

This penetrating comment goes to the heart of the matter and taking it as a useful starting point my initial problem of how best to develop my main theme - the relativity of all human 'values'- was partially resolved when I read William James views on the way temperament:-

'influenced which side of the fence philosophers come down deciding whether they are more hard-headed or more sentimental'.

For me this down-to-earth approach to philosophic and ethical questions helped to put the whole subject in a more realistic perspective for it brought out the relativity of everyone's (even philosophers'!) 'values', a view which Hamlet had put so succinctly many years before. This was the concept which had stayed with me ever since I first appreciated it leading to a view of ethical matters I had accepted as a simple fact of life. It was a view which the 'culture shock' I had experienced when I started to live and work in India had reinforced. It was, I believed, confirmed by my subsequent study and discussions.

At that time I read Sir Charles Sherrington's Gifford Lectures of 1937-8 in which he said:-

'While it is difficult to pin down just what individual 'values' are I suggest it is helpful if we consider them to be the result of our inherited character, our genes, worked upon by the 'values' we acquire, simple ones initially, from the adults who are responsible for our nurture and survival during our early dependent and most formative years.'

which highlighted the main issues in the argument I wanted to develop, namely that our unique individual and personal 'values' must, inevitably, be mainly of our own construction since we select, mostly subconsciously, those 'values' which best fit the genetic/biological patterns we have inherited.

In their departure from 'reality' (whatever that may be) such 'values' may well be ill-advised (in terms of our longer-term 'good') but from them we create the personal world, not the 'real' world, but the dream world in which we all live. We use them as a net to catch our impressions of other people, to formulate in our minds a working hypothesis of what other people want from us and how we can most effectively interact with them, to further our personal aims and interests as they are assessed by our personal 'values'. And all the time we are testing our view of life (as we see it through the inevitably distorting glass of those individual 'values') with the actuality as we experience it. Often refusing to accept that 'actuality' if it does not conveniently fit with our view of our relationship with other people.

The 'values' we acquire, those we 'catch' in the first year or so of our lives, continue to influence and, often to a material extent to determine, the personal 'rules' by which we continue to live. Subsequently other adults, the teachers in our schools, our ever-changing peers, the media in all its many forms and, even more powerfully, our own experiences will modify those initial values. Operating within the scope provided by our genetic/biological inheritance they decide how we assess ourselves and thus determine our relationships with others.

For me, Sherrington again put the essential features in their proper perspective, when he wrote:-

'Science, today, tells man he is a product of nature, a product of his planet and its sun. Even his mind which, at first, would seem to differentiate him from other forms of life is of the natural world. However he is the only part of life which glimpses things as a whole. He finds it more than just a whirlpool of energy without progress. There is a pattern but where this goes he cannot even guess...'

and

'Where have man's values come from? Whence has he got them? Inventions of his own? How can he trust them? Are they heritable? They are in the making. Man-made law has still to buttress them. He feels the curse as well as the blessing. The mill (evolution) he has emerged from produced a drive for survival which must now be tempered with 'values' calling for consideration for others...grappling with newly found values, yet with no experience but his own, no judgment but his own, no counsel but his own. Marked out it would seem to be a leader of life upon this planet with none to seek guidance from.'

- **Recent Research**

Since Sherrington's time, research particularly in genetics, biology and anthropology, has begun to indicate tentative, and partial, answers to his questions and, in Chapter 3, I have outlined some of them. It is an area where we are highly unlikely to achieve any degree of agreement until we can find a generally acceptable answer to the basic questions of the 'Why?' of the Universe and of the existence of conscious life on this minuscule planet. Our ignorance of the fundamental facts is summed up well by the comment that if our scientific knowledge should provide answers to every question of 'How?' and 'When?' we would still be left with the far more important question of 'Why?'

For the time being, therefore, we must be prepared to recognize the provisional nature of any view we may take unless we are willing to accept an answer based on faith or diktat alone.

- **A New Point of View?**

As my quotations from Sherrington show this is not an original approach but it is one which, it would seem, has largely been overlooked in recent years. The real advances we have made in understanding ourselves come primarily from discoveries about our minds, new approaches showing how we create our own personal cosmogony.

To the extent that concepts such as 'values' match the facts of life as we experience it they help us better to understand the complexities of our interrelationship with others. Such an approach will not solve all our problems but will, I suggest, encourage that tolerance the prime message about 'values' Jesus proclaimed and which, through the work of Paul and the other disciples, spread first through the Western World and then much further. It is a theme to be found in most of the other main religions and the ethical codes derived from them. But that is straying into the area of what 'values' ought to be which is not my primary concern here.

- **Actions Speak Louder Than Words**

In the Shorter Oxford Dictionary, VALUE (in this sense) is defined as -

> "Worthiness of persons in respect of... personal qualities".

This hints at, but does not fully convey, the sense of the word as I am using it. For years I have tried to establish a clear definition of what is commonly meant (and generally accepted) by the word 'values' when it is used in this context. In some ways it would seem to be associated with the meaning given by Plato when he used the Greek word which is commonly translated as 'virtues', not in the sense we use the word 'virtuous', but more as defining the essential quality of a human being, his or her 'character' and 'temperament', the personal factors which largely determine how other people interact with them.

These personal 'values' are not, it soon becomes evident, derived from any set of 'Absolutes' which can be rigidly defined and to which we should then aspire but are the rules, the internal discipline, we subconsciously use to relate to other people controlling and determining the way we act and interact. These 'values' are then the mental (influenced sometimes by physical) factors which, with our emotions, determine our perception of our 'interests' and therefore largely order our actions. Mostly they are NOT what the individual believes their 'VALUES' to be but are those concepts, ideas and feelings in both the conscious and unconscious mind which control the self-established and self-accepted rules which decide our actions when we have allowed (again consciously or unconsciously) for the interests and 'values' of others as we perceive them through the often distorting lens of our own 'values'. All these complex mental processes operating, mostly with but little conscious thought, in the flash of a second!

When considering how best to define what is meant by 'values' it is useful to recall that Wittgenstein held we should not look at a dictionary to see what a word really means but should study how it is used in different settings. Consider the terms 'values' and 'interaction of values' in this way, think how differently your 'values' (your principles?) operate when you are dealing with someone you love, your child for instance, as opposed to the way you assess the interests and 'values' of an arms length acquaintance. This, and the way your 'values' are then transformed into action, will give a better idea of the content of the word as I am using it and of the importance of the factor of interaction. If this lacks precision it must be recognized that many, if not most, of the basic concepts in modern physics - the 'hard' science - are equally imprecise and contain much that is difficult for the minds of the majority to visualize and comprehend.

Such individual 'values' are relative to time, place and circumstance and, above all, they are continuously influenced, as has already been said, by the need to interact with others' 'values' as we perceive them 'through a glass darkly'. For only a Robinson Crusoe (before Man Friday) or a complete anchorite could live entirely to himself ignoring all others. In Yorkshire they have a story which, to my mind, sums the position up very well - one old lady saying to another, 'Everyone's mad except thee and me and even thee's a bit queer'.

This brings out very clearly the uniqueness of individual 'values'. In that individuality they are like our fingerprints or DNA code for they are never exactly duplicated although they may well appear to be remarkably similar having common roots in our nature, our families and our culture.

- **Values derived from Religious Beliefs**

When the 'values' derived from the main religions and philosophies known to us are compared, it is evident that the emphasis each places on different 'virtues' (and therefore different 'values') differs widely. While there is usually common ground, the basic concepts of what is *'good'* and *'bad'*, what is *'right'* and *'wrong'* conduct, and of what is generally held to be *'fair'* and *'decent'* behaviour, differ so widely that what is really remarkable is not that there is so much misunderstanding and strife in the world but that there is not far more!

Humanity seems to be almost the only form of life which consistently kills, maims and tortures from 'principles' which stem from the 'values' we derive mainly from our inherited culture. There is another powerful saying - *'Ignorance is the mother of fear, and fear the evil godmother of cruelty'* the truth of which is demonstrated daily by our newspapers and television screens.

If humanity generally could accept that everyone has, and is entitled to, different 'values' then provided such personal 'values' conform reasonably to the laws and mores currently generally acceptable in the culture, and society, in which they live (i.e. such 'values' do not lead to behaviour materially threatening to another's way of life) there would be a better chance our children, and their children, would be able to live in a reasonably safe and civilized world. Surely it is the 'Absolutist' who is so certain he or she is 'right' who becomes willing, and indeed anxious, to convert the unbeliever (those who differ) to the 'true' faith who is found to be so ready to use violence, even extreme violence, to achieve their objectives by all the means available to them. Where cultures clash there is a greater, need for tolerance and here we come up against the more serious problem that on fundamental issues it is difficult to create a meeting of minds.

The 'ignorance' referred to in the quotation often stems from the very different 'values' derived from the powerful cultures derived from differing religious backgrounds. Understanding and appreciating legitimate differences becomes vitally important in any attempt to establish intra-cultural human-kindly laws and mores, a philosophy which often seems to be more in keeping with the Buddhist approach than any other except Christianity in its pristine form.

These matters are considered further in the Chapter on Ethics, Philosophies & Religions.

- **The Golden Bough**

Writing in the early part of this century Sir James Frazer pinpointed what must be a basic issue - how to determine the 'rights' of the individual when balanced against the 'responsibilities' necessary to maintain the cohesion of the group of which the individual is a member. He dealt at length with the part myths, and the concept of magic, played in humanity's earlier attempts to understand (and then to control) our environment both physical and human. In one section where he is dealing with the impact of Oriental religions on the West he says:-

Greek and Roman society was built on the conception of the subordination of the individual to the community...; it set the safety of the commonwealth as the supreme aim of conduct above the safety of the individual whether in this world or in a world to come...

and went on to point out how all this was changed by the spread of 'values' derived from Oriental religions which held that the direct communion of the individual with God (which such religions held to be the only route to eternal salvation in a predicated afterlife) was the sole objective worth living for.

It will be appreciated that from this particular approach comes the concept that it is the individual who is all important and not that individual's responsibility to the state. The now commonly held view that everyone is entitled to a 'fair' living provided by the State (i.e. other people) as opposed to the earlier concept that the individual had an obligation to contribute to the State (i.e. to the welfare of others) if he or she was to be entitled to support from others in case of need would seem to flow from this very different set of 'values'. And this is at the heart of one of the main debates in politics today, certainly in the Western world.

Taken to the limit the first approach is exemplified by totalitarianism, the Nazi/Fascist/Communist philosophy where

the State's interests (as determined by the ruling oligarchy) was dominant whereas the second approach postulates that it is the saint, the recluse disdainful of earth and rapt in ecstatic contemplation of God, which is the ideal to be aimed at.
In this, as in so much else, balance and tolerance of other's views are called for, the majority of individuals being required to accept that, to live in communities which provided the means by which they can survive and reproduce, they must play their part by accepting responsibilities to others as justification for claiming their rights as individuals.

- **The Pragmatic Approach to the Study of 'Values'**

The American philosopher William James stressing the importance of what he termed the pragmatic approach to philosophy wrote:-

'It (the pragmatic approach) *forbids us to rest content with a 'solving' name like 'God', 'Matter', 'Reason' ... Rather... You must bring out of each word its practical cash value, set it at work within your stream of experience. It appears then less as a solution than as a program for more work, and more particularly as an indication of the ways existing realities may be changed.'*

I fully accept this so the word 'values' must be just an introduction and not an answer, a beginning and not an end. In practice I have found this concept provides a useful tool in assessing the importance of much of what is being written on present day attitudes to science, philosophy and ethics.

- **How 'Values' Change**

We are subjected continuously, to pressures to change which, mostly, we ignore. Certainly after we have achieved some degree of 'maturity', most of us are remarkably conservative, holding to our existing 'values' unless and until some significant experience (such as an important change in our personal or cultural environment) produces sufficient pressure to cause us to alter. When we do change we try, unconsciously, to find a synthesis between the 'old' personal 'values' and the 'new' ones so that we can retain as much as possible of our earlier ideas with which we have been reasonably comfortable. What then determines significance? I suggest:-

'Any change in our 'values' which will, we believe, carry us readily from one part of our experience to another, linking our life satisfactorily with others, working securely, simplifying, such a modification is acceptable and then becomes 'true' for us.'

This does not necessarily mean we consciously decide what our 'values' should be (though perhaps we sometimes think we do!) nor indeed, in the longer run, do we always get the changes 'right' but usually, without conscious thought or deliberation, we absorb from the multitude of 'values' we are exposed to, the smorgasbord offered to us, those we instinctively feel will suit us, the selection being determined largely by inherited genetic factors. It can perhaps be likened to Jacob feeling comfortable in his 'coat of many colours' until, like a chameleon, he sensed a need to change to match new surroundings, or to adjust to new experiences. Mostly such changes come about subconsciously, comparatively rarely by design, a process somewhat akin, I suggest, to absorption by osmosis.

• What should we do?

Starting then with the assumption that in our lifetime it is highly unlikely we will even get a glimpse of 'Why' the Universe exists we need to find some kind of creed, some set of beliefs, which will provide a code, a set of 'values', enabling us to cope with the difficulties and tests of life, in order to survive and, if we so wish, pass on at least part of our 'values' to the succeeding generation.

Although I can advance no clear cut reason to justify my views, I prefer to believe the Universe is not a 'Cosmic Jest' and that there is some 'purpose' behind it. Whether that 'purpose' is comprehensible to us, here we are and here we must stay for the duration of our natural life. Therefore, our aim should I suggest be to live life to the full and to hand on our culture in good shape to our successors. To achieve these difficult (and sometimes apparently incompatible objectives) with due consideration for other people both of our culture and of others should be our prime objective.

As Iranaeus, one of the Saints, wrote:-

'The glory of God is man and woman fully alive'

and, as a general statement of the main objective in life, this could hardly be bettered but it does not provide the kind of effective moral yardstick we need in our ordinary daily life to help us judge how far we should allow our own 'values' and 'interests' to override the 'interests' and 'values' of others as we perceive them. Our own 'values' are the acid test which we must use providing the moral template to decide between 'right' ends and means, and to judge, in what circumstances, a 'right' end justifies a means which in other circumstances we would hold to be 'wrong'. This is the complex calculation we all make, mostly without conscious thought, many times each day.

Where then is the 'guidance' on which we can safely rely to judge the relative importance of the multitude of claims continuously made upon us particularly from those whom we love and have a responsibility for? How should we decide when 'to be fully alive' if it involves actions painful to those we love? Only our own 'values' will decide although we must be constrained, to a greater or lesser degree, by the mores of the culture and society in which we live.

In striving to pass such 'values' on particularly to children we must recognize that our own 'values' are themselves not 'Absolutes' and may well not suit the inherited qualities of our children nor be appropriate to the very different circumstances which, inevitably, they must experience. Circumstances which, because of the rapid rate of change inherent today particularly in Western societies, we may well find it difficult even to visualize.

- **Two Everyday Miracles**

Before I go on with the main theme I would like to draw attention to two everyday miracles we all take for granted - the first how a tiny fertilized cell develops, physically, into a human being and the other (an equally amazing fact) how that growing human being, starting from the fertilized cell, acquires the 'values' which seem to distinguish our form of life from all known others? How has biological inheritance been acted upon so that, within about twenty years, that microscopic egg becomes a fully functioning member of society and how, over a life span, can the individual's personality (as expressed in their 'values') adapt to such changing situations and roles while maintaining coherence and continuity?

- **The Main Issues**

The main issues I seek to investigate are:-

1. How an individual's 'values' determine their assessment of their personal 'interests' i.e.. how the interaction with others' 'values' (and perceived 'interests') influence action.

2. To what extent 'values' are 'caught rather than 'taught'.

3. How Nature and Nurture interact to form an individual's 'values' and the part formal education plays in influencing the outcome.

4. How 'values' are communicated by 'body' and other language.

5. How our lack of knowledge of the purpose of the Universe and of the reason for conscious life on this minuscule planet requires us 'to take a view', consciously or unconsciously, on the myths put forward by our culture and religion.

6. How this ignorance of the fundamental reasons for our existence makes it impossible to establish Absolutes which would then provide real and effective guidance helping us to decide just how to deal with the often complex and confusing issues of today's existence.

and finally

7. How we can best establish a set of 'values' which would appeal sufficiently to the world's widely differing cultures and religions so that we may have a reasonable chance of our children and grandchildren avoiding nuclear or other genocide.

I am fully aware that this raises many questions beyond my competence to answer, and that what I have written can only be regarded as an introduction, a minor contribution to the major ethical problems involved. The approach has, I consider, the virtue of some originality, throwing light as it does upon the need for an appreciation of the way 'values' originated, how they are acquired and how they are continuously transmuted. To seek some kind of an answer to these vital questions has indeed been a fascinating quest.

The next chapter attempts to consider what are the essential factors in determining individual 'values', to bring out the relative importance of the factors of inheritance and training, between 'nature' and 'nurture', in the formation of those 'values' but before moving on I want to draw particular attention to one important aspect which such a study of how 'values' are established must have for us in these rapidly changing times.

- **Is The Dominance of Western Cultural 'Values' Ending?**

For much of the last two hundred years Western cultural 'values' have been spreading, and largely dominating, many of the 'values' derived from other cultures largely because of the success of the Scientific Method (developed in the West) in providing mankind with an increasing dominance over our environment. This has been enhanced by the rapid growth of communication techniques derived from that scientific revolution which have made it ever easier to pass those Western 'values' on.

Western ideas now rule as never before. Its economic and military might still stand unrivalled. Most governments pay at least lip-service to liberal democracy which is now the commonly accepted ideal of 'good' government. The World Bank and the International Monetary Fund can readily be regarded as the modern instruments of colonialism and, for many people, modernization has so far been mentally equated with the acceptance, and adoption, of Western cultural 'values'.

However these outstanding successes of Western culture are associated with self-evident internal problems and decline. Civic bonds are weakening, many of the basic ideas such as the acceptance of duties and responsibilities in return for 'rights' are being abrogated and, in the West, political leadership often seems to be absent or misguided. The Cold War consensus on collective security has gone and military spending is declining dramatically (probably itself a major factor in the economic slowdown) even as much of the rest of the world erupts. The old Paulian 'work ethic' is being superseded, in part, by a Confucian concept which treats 'work' as a necessary evil appropriate for some members of the body politic only.

While the West moves towards disarmament others around the world are busy developing nuclear or other mass weapons so that soon (in an historic sense) the majority of nuclear-weapon states could be non-Western. A world in which a dictator such as a Hitler, a Gaddaffi or a Saddam Hussein could have the capacity effectively to threaten atomic or bacteriological war against Europe and the US would be vastly different to the one we now know.

In the Confucian and Islamic cultures there are two growing challengers to the West. Islam is expanding beyond its original heartland and with the emancipation of Muslim republics in the former Soviet Union is likely to pose an increasing threat particularly as it controls so much of the world's reserves of oil and other natural power resources. In Africa it is expanding south of the Sahara to such an extent that Zambia has felt forced to declare itself a Christian state. Through immigration Islam has established a foothold in France and elsewhere in Europe while proving itself largely immune to the absorption of community 'values' from the West. Theocracy (which, rationally, was supposed to give way to democracy) has proved in Islamic cultures to be surprisingly resilient.

However the most serious challenger to the West lies, probably, in the Pacific rim where the Confucian bloc has the great advantage of ever increasing numbers. The educated in those countries no longer necessarily serve as promoters of Western ideas and 'values' and often seem, in Western eyes at any rate, to be reverting to their earlier fundamental 'values' which differ materially from those our own culture tends to inculcate.

So it is beginning to be questionable to what extent Western ideas and 'values' still have their earlier persuasive force. Indeed can the Western 'myth' survive now the Russian Communist threat has diminished if not disappeared? To what extent did the 'red menace' act as a social glue binding the West together? What is there left to rally around? Liberal democracy and modified capitalism? Hardly the stuff to encourage wholehearted resistance to rampant nationalism showing either Islamic or Confucian colours.

While the concept of collective duties and responsibilities reigns largely unchallenged in other parts of the world, the West is continuously stressing the importance of individual rights and 'values'. Both the Islamic and Confucian cultures are inspired by faith in their individual cultural values while the West, mostly nominally Christian, has largely lost religion as a guiding principle so that, deep down, its identity appears to be becoming ever more shallow. And this change could well be encouraged by the tolerance of other faiths its prime message conveys.

While the global conflict was one of competing ideologies the West was on firm ground but now the conflict is becoming one of cultural 'values' it finds it much more difficult to resist. Just as the Roman Empire thought its technological superiority must protect it from the Barbarians so we may be making much the same mistake if we do not carefully examine, and understand, that cultural 'value' conflict could well be the basis of the next World revolution.

Chapter 2

Nature & Nurture

"...to thine own self be true..." (Hamlet) Shakespeare

To 'know thyself' must be one of the more difficult maxims to follow. Most people spend the first twenty or thirty years of their lives trying to find out just what abilities and qualities the genetic roulette of the sexual process has dealt them and all the while that initial raw material is being manipulated, and polished, by their experiences at home and abroad.

In human development the relative importance of 'nature' and 'nurture', of inheritance and environment has been debated for many years and no conclusion has been reached. As more is learned about the complexity of the way the brain functions and of the mental processes themselves this seems only to complicate the question still further. Currently the consensus seems to give increasing weight to genetic factors with nurture being regarded as a modifying process, a 'polishing agent', something which 'brings out the grain in the wood' but does not alter the inherent nature of the 'wood' i.e. the original character, itself. Almost certainly the influence of these two factors varies from one individual to another.

- **Basic Factors**

To survive and to reproduce, all living organisms must show

two contradictory properties. They must retain a reasonable degree of stability - specificity - during development and into adult life, resisting the pressures of the endless buffeting of environmental changes and they must also show plasticity, the ability to adapt and to modify this specificity by recognizing the need for change, and then translating that recognition into suitable modifications, internalizing the realities of life as they are experienced.

What earlier would probably have been described as an interplay between genes and environment is now, by many biologists, regarded as a somewhat simplistic view since it is an individual's genes which provide the main basis for both specificity and plasticity. So, when considering how 'values' are 'caught' rather than 'taught', while those derived from nurture and training will, it now seems generally agreed, be strongly influenced (if not determined) by genetic inheritance, nurture and training will, it is held, materially affect how those 'caught' values are expressed in terms of action, reaction and interaction.

For us then our 'values', derived culturally and 'caught' individually, must show much the same qualities i.e. they must show both specificity and plasticity. As we know from experience the impact of the two factors varies widely with different individuals and, indeed, with each person with time and circumstance.

In an attempt to assess the differing effects of 'nature' and 'nurture' a variety of studies have been made (often concentrating on the development of identical and other twins who have been separated at birth), but no final conclusion has yet been reached. One elaborate analysis of the whole range of information available in this area (*'Genes, Culture and Personality'* published in 1989 by Eaves, Eysenck and Martin) confirmed the importance of heredity while recognizing that the acquisition of 'values' necessarily took place within the ambit of the culture and the family.

Speaking of the development of 'values', Sir Charles Sherrington, in his valuable book, 'Man on his Nature', wrote:-

'He (the human) reflects that at one time the planet can have had none of his particular species of system. Now it has. That is, it has evolved recognizable mind... The planet has thus, latterly, become a place for thinking. More it now recognizes values as 'values'. It is a planet now with hopes and fears and tentative 'right' and 'wrong'.'

Then, following a section in which he considered what he cited as probably the fundamental value - whether, and to what extent, human life should be regarded as 'sacred' - came:-

'(with the coming of man) the situation has changed. The rule and the scene are there and are the same apart from himself. The change is in himself. Where have his values come from? ...For all other forms of life 'wrong' is. .impossible.. equally impossible is 'right'. (then writing of man's 'values') *'Whence has he got them? Inventions of his own? How far can he trust them? Can 'a priori' principles suffice to base them? Are they heritable?'*

- **Derivation of Individual 'Values'**

Consider the way 'values' are acquired and develop at the various stages of our growth and experience:-

- **Earliest Development**

In the way they acquire their earliest 'values' growing children seem to mimic the manner in which, over the many thousands of years of Homo sapiens existence, 'values' have developed largely by trial and error. These 'values' enabled humanity to live in family, and then in larger groups, mostly in reasonable harmony, providing the essential succour and protection enabling (some of) the children to survive to maturity and to reproduce.

Eventually as control over the environment was increased this led to the larger groups and civilizations with their disparate mores, customs and values.

- **Individual 'Values'**

For babies the ability to distinguish a 'right' from a 'wrong' action must initially be derived from the adults who make their survival possible. What is 'good' for those adults becomes initially 'right' and what they say is 'bad' becomes 'wrong'. Later more sophisticated 'values' are acquired some from the parents, some from other adults (such as their wider family, their teachers, writers, preachers, politicians and family friends), some from their peers and others from the media in its many forms.

We know that, in forms of life other than human, incredibly complex instincts are inherited. To the extent that this is true of humans such inheritance provides the 'qualities' which form the original material on which exposure works to produce the 'values' which will, to a material extent, determine how each individual will assess the importance of his or her 'interests', how they will interact with others and which will then broadly determine their behaviour.

For each of us our inherited 'qualities' are unique, our personal 'interaction' with our early human environment is unique and, therefore, our resulting 'values' must be unique. Thus we each carry our own personal 'yardsticks' for assessing 'right' and 'wrong' which conform, to a greater or lesser degree, with the commonly accepted standards set by the 'culture' of our particular society.

- **'Values' are Caught not Taught**

This is a fundamental proposition - that our inherited genetic factors determine the extent to which, individually, we are able to 'catch on' to the various concepts which, in each culture, establish what is generally and currently regarded as 'fair', 'reasonable', 'decent' and 'seemly'.

Many human features are distributed among the overall population according to 'the normal distribution curve' and it seems at least possible that the spread of such genetic factors follows broadly the same pattern. If this theory is sound it becomes likely that, while the great majority in each generation will be able to 'catch' those commonly accepted and approved 'values', there will be the individuals at the ends of the distribution (what is sometimes called the lunatic fringe) who will not and it is these who provide the demons, or the saints, to whom the normal rules of behaviour simply do not apply.

These will almost inevitably contravene the basic laws, rules and mores which each community establishes to maintain its form and to perpetuate itself and its culture. This theme is developed in a later Chapter.

• The Biological Origin of some 'Values'

Dr. Margaret Gruter in her book 'Law and the Mind' has provided a valuable insight into the biological origins of some human behaviour and therefore, of some of our 'values'. She emphasized that modern behavioural science, particularly evolutionary biology and ethology (the study of animal behaviour), have now disposed of the simplistic concept of *'nature red in tooth and claw'* and have instead revealed the crucial themes of co-operation and altruism elucidating how these have helped to introduce new `values` which, in time, enabled humans to live together successfully in larger and more complex social groups.

Thus modern research is beginning to propose empirical answers to some of the questions about the source and nature of many human 'values'. A crucial question is, obviously, what relevance has animal behaviour to human 'qualities' (and therefore to human 'values')? Dr. Gruter proposes that, like all other forms of life, humans are initially 'programmed' by genetic inheritance toward certain behaviour patterns by evolutionary 'grain' so that it needs special incentives and constraints to make people act contrary to such 'programming'. She suggests there are two opposing 'drives' one selfish and aggressive and the other loving and altruistic. 'Law' and 'mores' are human devices to mediate between them. She lays stress upon our responsibility to future generations, namely our obligation to ensure the survival of our species (and our set of 'values'), and emphasizes that this should be recognized as the main task facing us.

If her approach is accepted (and personally I consider it reasonable to do so), a more effective approach to the question of the origin of human 'values' seems likely if the importance of the biological factors is granted (as indicated also in the Eaves, Eysenck and Martin analysis). 'Values', a product of the human mind, are a by-product of the biological mechanisms which support, and make possible, the human quest for order and for fairness. Therefore an understanding of evolutionary biology (associated with a study of early human cultural achievements) may well provide vital clues in helping us to understand the origins of some of our more basic 'values'.

An equally important factor is the recognition of the perpetual conflict between competition and continuity in achieving what we 'perceive' to be our 'interests'. These two basic drives tend to appear to us as aggression and co-operation and how the conflict is resolved is determined primarily by each individual's unique 'values'.

Humans, the most versatile and adaptive of the primates, find a common ground in their need for order and equity (Note. The word 'fairness' rather than 'equity' may better express the basic concept). Studies of child development, especially the origin of spoken words and gestures, and the way a child acquires a command of language (enabling and encouraging interaction of `values`), all emphasize the need for 'rules' and 'laws' helping us mentally to impose some kind of order on the chaotic-seeming world we first experience as a baby.

This means that the absorption of personal 'values' (which include rule making, rule incorporating and rule obeying) is an integral part of every individual's development some finding the aggressive drive more imperative while others lean more towards cooperation. A small proportion find it impossible to absorb the concept that, for society's sake, they must allow for, and interact with, other's 'reasonable' interests and 'values'.

The concept that basic human 'values' have a largely biological origin in no way implies that such 'values' (and therefore our consequent behaviour) are fixed (as instincts are largely fixed) since experience and learning will continuously influence and modify the 'values' which control that behaviour. Recent research, while emphasizing the 'plasticity' of behaviour among most species and indicating that many forms of behaviour are caused by genetic inheritance, still indicates that such genetic inheritance often sets limits to the degree of 'plasticity'.

There would, therefore, seem to be sound arguments for accepting a biological origin for many of our basic 'values'. Such as the compulsion most adults feel to help protect the young whether their own or others. More generally to recognize a communal sense of 'fairness' which expresses an overall acceptance of a 'reasonable' balance between their 'rights' and 'obligations'.

- **Community of 'Values'**

However what one society considers 'fair', 'just' and 'reasonable' does not apply universally. Nevertheless, underlying the obvious cultural differences, there are common biological factors leading to cross cultural agreement on what is 'fair' and what is not in particular biological conditions. To quote a specific instance in most cultures preference is given to the mother rather than to the father for the custody of young children if there is a marital rift.

- **Genes, Culture and Personality**

In the book mentioned earlier (by Eaves, Eysenk and Martin) there is a wealth of information which has been analysed in an attempt to provide a statistical basis for the relative importance of inheritance and training/experience. The single outstanding conclusion was that no one model satisfactorily explained the variation and transmission of every characteristic they studied. While in almost every case models based on genetic effects fitted the results better it would be a gross oversimplification to conclude that the data for each variable could be summarized adequately by classical heritability estimates. The usual assumptions in genetic models for behaviour did not capture all the nuances of the individual differences the authors had found. As the samples became larger (and included more diverse kinds of relationship) the simple genetic model needed modification particularly in the case of the study of the degree of similarity between twins.

The authors considered two possibilities (both dependent on genetic effects), the first that 'extraversion' (one of the traits they studied in depth) was itself the result of genes displaying non-additive interactions, the second that there are competitive social interactions between the two twins so that a twin who is genetically predisposed to 'extraversion' will thus create an 'introverting' environment for a co-twin.

Just how this interaction works is a matter of conjecture but it could well be that the drive for a particular 'niche' in the family during growing up means the 'sociable' child gets the 'friends' leaving the 'books' to his more introverted sibling. With the available data it was impossible to make any realistic decision in favour of one view or the other.

An important observation dealt with the difference in the causes of 'extraversion' compared with 'introversion'. Repeatedly the authors found the competitive factor associated with extraversion is not found for such traits as neuroticism. The authors say the evidence supports the original distinction made between extraversion and neuroticism as indices of two distinct and independent processes underlying personality development. These two 'super factors' displayed quite different patterns of genetic and environmental causation.

- **Social Attitudes**

The major surprise in the analyses was, curiously enough, the strong indication of a genetic component in variations in social attitudes although no simple relationship between genetic inheritance and particular social attitudes had been found. In Western type societies in particular, the opportunities for social interaction offered are nowadays so varied that each individual is faced with a 'smorgasbord' of 'values' competing for acceptance. Such 'values' are, of course, derived mainly from parents, teachers, peers and the media.

Any model for 'social' learning must provide for the fact that each individual begins life with their own 'agenda' in terms of different sensitivities to particular kinds of social reward. In the context of personality, individual 'sensitivity parameters' are likely to be determined genetically rather than socially and the data suggested there may well be an overall genetic tendency for some to be 'radical' rather than 'conservative' as expressed in the terms used in Western societies.

The last main point is that the relative effects of genes and environment would seem to differ according to sex. Not all the genes seeming to affect the personality in one sex automatically affect the other in the same way. The sexes would, in general, seem to differ appreciably in their degree of sensitivity to social environment and in their reaction to social pressure.

- **Indoctrination**

Traditionally the development of 'values' has been regarded as primarily a matter of 'indoctrination' with the greatest influence being that which gets more of the individual's time and offers him/her the greatest 'reward'. The authors say this is an oversimplification because it ignores the unique role of inherited preferences and sensitivity in filtering, choosing and acquiring the information from the particular environment which goes a long way to mould character.

- **The Human Environment**

Reverting now to the way the environment (particularly the human environment) affects the growing child:-

- **Infancy**

In a normal newly-born baby there are physical instincts and reflexes (such as the instinct to suckle) which are apparent almost from birth and which are an essential factor for the survival of the baby and, therefore, of the species. During the first year the brain grows very fast enabling the infant to absorb (and mentally to organize) an enormous amount of information. By about six weeks the baby has learned to smile and at four months it is laughing and giggling. During the first year the baby gradually comes to feel more complicated emotions such as jealousy, petulance and affection. In these vitally important formative first twelve months, foundations are laid for many types of adult behaviour, emotions and skills so that basic inherited 'qualities' then start to be modified.

At birth, the infant is solely concerned with its own survival; its interests are overwhelmingly self-centred, designed to ensure survival at all costs and it is not until other 'values' have been acquired that a concern for others emerges. Later other genetic factors come into play and the expression of these factors begins to be modified by interaction with the 'values' of others, particularly the parents or other adults who are providing the sustenance and protection essential for the infant to survive. Such interaction will normally start with the 'values' of the mother or, failing her, of the other adult(s) responsible for the child's early survival and well-being.

Gradually the wholly self-centred 'values' are modified by other influences and the child learns, in some cases quite rapidly, to be concerned with the well-being of others.

Conceptual development starts from the time a child first begins to understand actions and spoken words or noises. It continues throughout life (except for some at the oldest ages) as there is a growing need to deal with all kinds of problems involving abstract ideas from the simple to the complex. Throughout these early years (between one and four) emotions can change dramatically as the child discovers its individuality. After four, emotions tend to fluctuate less and at this age most children start to play and to share happily with other children. By five 'values' are usually sufficiently formed for some children to show considerable concern and responsibility in looking after younger children particularly, of course, those of the same family group.

- **Childhood**

At five a child's grasp of abstract ideas is usually based upon simple comparisons such as 'hotter', 'younger', and 'more'. At seven the child will slowly learn to take decisions and solve problems based upon logic rather than guesswork, by ten they should have a thorough grasp of ideas involving time and by twelve a normal child should be able to reason on a simple scale in much the same way as an adult. Young children tend to react badly to anything which upsets them deeply such as parental discord or losing physical or mental stability in another way (e.g. moving house, going to a new school or emigrating).

Children's values are often strongly influenced by their peers and they will sometimes goad one another into behaviour they know is generally unacceptable to the adults who sustain and control them. They may go through a phase when they deliberately do the things they have been taught not to do, lying, cheating, fighting and swearing which often stem from an unconscious desire to test, and thus establish, the disciplinary framework surrounding them which provides the security essential for them. Thus they rebel to test the real 'values' of the adults who provide that security, a good example of an early 'interaction of values'.

Given that, at the earlier ages, the attitudes and reasoning of those adults must be almost if not quite incomprehensible to the child and, given also, their normal instinct to mimic, and to placate, the adults who control them, the natural strong feelings of dependence can, in some cases, cause a guilty feeling in the child because adult attitudes (deriving from their 'values') run contrary to much, if not all, of the child's natural biological behaviour.

This feeling of guilt can, in turn, reinforce the feeling of dependency thus creating a continuous chain of unwitting offence against adult 'values' with a consequent need for absolution. For a time this can enhance the strength of the family authoritarian relationship which only weakens as the child develops and recognizes that its own developing interests and 'values' have for it a special validity in its own particular, still largely self-centred, world.

Perhaps the most effective way of weakening the child's will is to arouse, and to stimulate, their sense of 'guilt' by making the child continually conscious of the way its natural behaviour is contrary to generally acceptable adult 'values'. In Western societies most children are taught from their earliest days that their natural functions and sexual strivings need to be suppressed or diverted into more socially acceptable forms and when, inevitably, the child transgresses the guilt feeling is usually increased once again.

When such a relationship between sexual, and other natural urges, and 'guilt' has been established in the child's mind, a powerful association has been built up between the two and by the age of five or six it seems many children have acquired a pervasive sense of guilt because of the conflict between their natural impulses and the adults' 'values' as shown by their, the adult's, public actions and speech.

(It is worth noting that rebellion, the child's natural reaction to the pressure of parental 'values', has been suggested as a more natural basis for Freud's 'Oedipus Complex' than the sexual jealousy he put forward as the primary cause).

Later as the child matures and becomes more aware of their own 'values', rebellion can lead to the kind of family friction which is a commonplace in the adolescent years when the maturing youngster becomes more and more susceptible to the pressure of the 'values' of their peers. In our rapidly changing

Western societies these are often worlds apart from those regarded as acceptable to (and convenient for!) the older generations who are normally still largely in control.

• Violence and Cruelty

In her book 'The Drama Of Being A Child' the psychoanalyst Dr. Alice Miller has drawn attention to the factors in conventional child rearing and education which can encourage the violence and cruelty that are so prevalent in society. She emphasizes that many children feel constrained to adapt from birth to the needs and ambitions of their parents so that in some cases they largely lose the ability to experience and express their true feelings and therefore eventually become estranged from their real selves.

In one section of her book she brings out the important point that, within a culture which is shielded from other 'value' systems (such as that of orthodox Jewry in the ghetto), an adapted individual was often not autonomous, lacking in some part, their own individual sense of identity and relying instead on the support provided by the group. The framework provided by being a 'devout Jew' gave individuals a measure of security which otherwise they would have lacked in their often alien environment.

Today, particularly in the Western world, it is far more difficult to be insulated from other groups with different 'values' so that the unquestioning acceptance of a body of ideas and 'values' (such as Orthodox Jewry provided) is much more difficult to maintain. Individuals are therefore thrown back on to their own resources having to rely upon their personal 'values' which have been basically formed early in life.

Dr. Miller goes on to suggest that the conflict of 'values' often experienced by children because of fractured parental relationships (and who may, therefore, well have lacked an early loving and secure background) could contribute to the rapid increase of depression as an illness in more recent times. In this sense of the word, 'depression' can perhaps be likened to the Christian sin of 'accidie' - the opposite of that zest for life which, surely, it should be our ambition to achieve enabling us to live life to the full while, at the same time, striving to cause the minimum of hurt to others.

Dr. Miller summed her conclusions up thus;-

"For their development children need the respect and protection of adults who take them seriously, love them and honestly help them to become adjusted to the world they are living in. (In other words help them to acquire appropriate 'values'). *If these vital needs are not met then the children are likely to have their integrity impaired. The normal reaction of the child would be anger and pain but in this kind of hurtful environment the child is usually forced to suppress their feelings so that later it will usually be found they have no memory of what was done to them."*

This often leads to destructive acts against others (behaviour typical, I may add, of the 'maladjusted' boys at the special School where I am a Governor) and, when these children become parents themselves, they will often unwittingly direct acts of revenge against their own children whom they subconsciously treat as scapegoats. Such forms of child abuse (in the guise of child-rearing) is, in many Western Cultures, not only acceptable but often encouraged. Such parents sometimes beat their children to release the emotions derived from the sufferings of their own childhood.

If maltreated children are not to become mentally ill, drug addicted or criminals it is essential that, at least once in their lives, they should find an adult who will accept them as they are thus showing they are not irredeemably labelled as 'wicked' and that that adult believes in him or her as a person.

There is a view, still prevalent in some sections of Western society, that most children are crafty creatures dominated by wicked drives who tell lies, attack their 'innocent' parents (or desire them sexually). It is this view which is largely to blame for a set of adult 'values' justifying the treatment of children as naturally sinful whereas if adults were to base their approach to children on the need to inculcate 'values' expressing love and respect this should materially help to prevent the development of many of the twisted personalities which today give rise to so much mental illness and antisocial behaviour.

- **Adolescence**

This is when the child becomes an adult physically, a process which involves basic changes, for which the individual's 'values' may well not be ready. Muscles, the brain and the central nervous system all virtually complete all their physical development. Major psychological changes take place as the individual begins to face up to the responsibilities of adulthood, nowadays often gaining financial independence and, at the same time, having to come to terms with their maturing bodies and sexual development.

Often their personality can become very unlovable and the parents, or other adults involved, need to exercise all the tolerance they are capable of while the awkward stage is worked through. Hormonal changes can cause sudden and apparently inexplicable changes of mood which can puzzle and trouble the youngster just as much as they do the rest of the family or group.

In Western society the adolescent is usually still expected to accept a degree of parental and school discipline while being charged, at the same time, with being self-motivated about work, being responsible in dealing with money, alcohol and drugs and for controlling sexual relationships. All this tumult almost inevitably involves changes, sometimes dramatic ones, in the adolescent's interests, 'values' and attitudes.

For most these are usually temporary and, in later perspective, minor problems but for some they cause serious disturbances leading to such illnesses as anorexia nervosa, to periodic depression, to alcohol or drug addiction and, in extreme cases, to attempted or to actual suicide. In such cases the adolescent's inherited qualities and acquired 'values' will be tested to the limit if not beyond.

Social problems arise also from the adolescent's natural desire for sexual discovery and experiment, for independence and for rebellion against parental and other adult 'values' and control. They are more likely to occur when the individual's perception of their condition (which is itself largely decided by their individual 'values') becomes remote from reality and when the adolescent feels left on their own with no-one they feel they can safely turn to, someone with the necessary experience and wisdom, to advise them sympathetically and realistically.

Today, in Western societies, the main areas of adolescent social problems are usually concerned with sex (sexual diseases and unwanted pregnancies), drug abuse and crime. As a prophylactic against these a 'balanced' set of 'values' is needed and these must largely have been acquired by the example and practice of the adults they respond to and respect and, in some cases, by the example of their peers.

- **Adulthood**

As they develop into adults, most adolescents become more conscious of the way their perceived interests, and now more formed 'values', interact and often conflict with those who have varying degrees of control over them whether they be parents, teachers or those, such as the police, who are called upon to represent, and to enforce, the 'values' of the culture and society in which they are living. The reaction of a substantial proportion of youngsters often takes the form of rebellion which may well be another example of experiment testing the limits, discovering how far their interests and 'values' can influence, or dominate, the adults on whom, at least some young people, still have to remain dependent. This applies particularly in those social classes which, by habit and convention, require the adolescents to go through an extended period of further education or training.

This means that such youngsters often cannot be self-supporting until they are well over the age when they are conscious of the fact they are fully adult with all the urges, needs and often responsibilities natural to that state. Earlier 'values' derived from their parents and their original peers are being modified (sometimes quite dramatically) by the different 'values' they are now more exposed to, at university or at other forms of Higher education, and particularly nowadays from the media. This tension between two different roles, that of the dependent while wanting to be independent, should normally have a maturing effect as the subtleties of learning to resolve the multiple interactions of 'values' are learned by experiment and experience. It is a stage many have to go through (whether at university or elsewhere) although for some the modern pattern of remuneration means they can be self-supporting at a far earlier age than was true prior to World War Two.

Some make the passage to adulthood easily others find it far more difficult but it does not seem to be necessarily true that the difficult ones in their 'teens' are necessarily less successful as human beings when they become adults.

Physical adulthood begins when the genetic program of physical growth is completed, the mental will take much longer. During early adulthood personal motivation is usually at its strongest. A young adult will usually be keen to establish a successful social role and a career, to start to build satisfactory emotional and sexual relationships and generally to define and start to fulfil ambitions. It is the time to find out what particular gifts have been received in the genetic roulette game if this has not already been made clear from earlier experience.

So, providing the right opportunities are available, most young adults tend to be ambitious, enthusiastic and dedicated whether in choosing the 'right' partner, rearing children or in pursuing a career. A time when for most, the zest for life comes freely and easily. At this stage they are utilizing the 'value skills' they have acquired seeking to secure their interests and relating to a growing number of people. If these natural objectives and needs are thwarted there may well be a rebellion against socially acceptable 'values' leading to drugs, alcoholism and crime.

Emotional maturity normally lags way behind physical maturity since the often crude existing 'values' need to be modified and smoothed by the experience which can only be found in the complexities of the adult world. Some are fortunate because by inheritance, or by earlier training, their 'values' are already sufficiently 'mature' to be able to adjust readily to the wider sphere they are now entering. Some sadly never do learn how to adjust to the interests and 'values' of others, even those close to them, and they remain for ever in 'the awkward squad'.

- **Starting to Work**

There is a break, often of a traumatic kind, when youngsters start to work and this may well be more pronounced if they join one of the Services. Suddenly they must adjust to a whole new set of 'values' which, broadly speaking, they must accept without question even if, from their earlier training and experience, many of the new 'values' seem alien or even, at times, absurd. In some of the service situations they would, on occasion, appear to be almost inhuman.

Being catapulted into a very different environment can be a severe testing time but, constructively handled, the experiences should stand the individual in good stead in later years. He or she must learn to interact with the 'values' of their new colleagues modifying their own behaviour, learning what they must do to enable them to live reasonably comfortably in their new circumstances or, if they find they cannot do this, they must break away and seek a new milieu. The basic choice is to adjust or to move, to fight or to fly.

So, if they stay, they must learn to cope, to learn when to show feelings and when to hide them, when to maintain a point of view and when to defer. They will learn that the true hierarchy of the organization is, more often than not, quite different from the officially accepted view because of the different characters ('values') of the people in the positions of major or minor power. If they are lucky, they will find an older and more experienced colleague who will help them to appreciate these other important adult 'values' and whose example will provide a good guide when similar problems are met in later years.

- **Further Education**

Going on to study at a University, or at a college for further education, (preferably not directly from school but after at least a year in the outside world) is another exposure to different 'values' which should modify the earlier sometimes simplistic 'values' derived from home and from school. That year in the outside world should help to avoid fixing the type of 'values' which can so readily come from staying too long in 'the ivory tower' milieu and the wider experience of the 'real' world should also help to encourage a greater tolerance of others' interests and 'values'.

- **The 'Ivory Tower' Syndrome**

The constricting effect of staying solely in an 'Ivory Tower' milieu is brought out admirably by the following quotation from Len Deighton's novel 'Sinker' (in which he likens education at Oxbridge to a shell). One of his characters speaking indirectly of 'values' says;-

'You and I belong to a class obsessed by the notion of conduct. At our best public schools we have always taught young men that 'service' is the highest calling. Service to God, to our

Sovereign, Service to our Country. I'm simply saying that Bernard's background, the boys he grew up with and his family, have another priority. For them, and who is to say they are wrong, loyalty to the family comes before everything else and I mean EVERYTHING.

An Oxbridge education can make graduates feel they are members of some privileged elite destined to lead and make decisions which are inflicted on lesser beings. Such elitism must of necessity be based on expectations which are often not fulfilled. Thus Oxbridge has not only provided Britain with its most notable politicians and Civil servants but also with its most embittered spies...

Bernard's arrogance comes from something inside him; some vital force and a seemingly inexhaustible fund of courage. Our great universities will never be able to furnish inner strength, no one can. What teachers provide is always superimposed upon the person who is something that already exists. Education is a carapace, a cloak laid upon the soul, a protection or something to hide inside.'

That seems to me an excellent illustration of the issues in the continuing 'nature' versus 'nurture' debate providing a useful lead in to the educational process which is dealt with at greater length in Chapter 4 and the Appendix. By the time a youngster reaches university the fundamental 'values' may well be largely formed but perhaps not hardened. What happens at university decides, at least in part, the final 'polish'.

- **Pairing and Marriage**

For most of us this is one of the most dramatic changes in life, that of learning to live closely by, and to interact intimately with, a partner, usually of the opposite sex. Someone with a different, sometimes a very different, background and often with materially different 'values' and 'interests'. One of the outstanding features of almost all Western societies is the overriding emphasis put upon the emotional/romantic and sexual side of such relationships which must surely be one of the main reasons for the high incidence of divorce. And since divorce statistics relate only to marriage (no record being kept of the many other long-term relationships which break up) they probably show only the tip of the iceberg.

The social implications, particularly those arising in one parent families, are a major cause of further communal problems at least partly because of the inevitably limited 'values' which are transmitted from the sole parent to the child. In a normal two-parent family a child learns from the beginning to recognize that the adults providing the essential sustenance and protection have different, sometimes conflicting, 'values' which is a valuable experience usually helping them to adjust more readily to the realities of the adult world.

If the simple fact that each individual has, and is entitled to, their own interests and 'values' was generally accepted and became a part of the 'values' taught at home and at school and if this was associated with a recognition of the way that, continuously, those complex 'values' must interact if zest in life is to be maintained for both individuals, this should go a long way to help to resolve many of the inevitable differences and conflicts arising from disparate family, cultural and educational backgrounds.

- **Absolutes**

If we have learned to accept that no-one has yet been able to establish generally acceptable definitions of Absolutes, that there are legitimate differences of opinion as to 'good' and 'bad', 'right' and 'wrong' arising from assessments which vary according to differing interests and 'values', the ground rules in the family for tolerance of others' 'values' and opinions should more readily be established.

Obviously there must be limits to such tolerance and these limits must generally be established by society and interpreted by the individuals according to their circumstances. The prime function of religious teachers and philosophers should be to help us establish how those limits ought to be defined to ensure that the two parent family is maintained as the primary mode and that our form of culture and social organization survives and prospers.

So, in marriage or in any other pairing, each adult has to learn how to adjust and modify their 'values' to deal with anger, tiredness, pleasure, frustration, jealousy, physical attraction and many other emotions. The individuals concerned may well have attained physical maturity but emotional maturity will, in most cases, take much longer and may well never be achieved.

- **Middle Age Crises**

A good deal has been written about middle age crises which, for many women, often start with the fact that the children they had when they were first married in their early twenties have grown up and left home and that, as yet, there are no grandchildren to take their place. Alternatively, men and women who have concentrated on a career can become conscious that they have failed to achieve their ambitions (or they are dissatisfied with the results) and that, at their age, the opportunities for future growth and development seem to have disappeared. At such a time unless they have broadly based 'values' to sustain them they can become embittered losing the zest for life which is vital in helping to sustain a happy and rewarding life.

- **Changes in Family Relationships**

Human infants require a long period of dependency on adults before they can survive by their own efforts. This fundamental biological fact has, necessarily, a dominant influence on human 'values'. There is usually a clear cut change in family relationships when a child is borne since the male partner has to accept the fact that while, in most families, he may well be the central providing factor, his mate's attitude (determined by her 'values' biological and other) are likely to change, sometimes quite dramatically. For a time, at least, the man's importance, his ranking in the family hierarchy, will have to take second place to the needs, usually clamorous ones, of the new baby.

This is, of course, a generalization but the coming of a child, particularly of a first child, provides a jump, a discontinuity in relationships which usually causes some significant changes in interactions and, given the strength of the maternal 'instinct' in most women, this leads quite often to material changes in the apparent 'values' of the mother with the partner often taking some time to adjust. The parents now have to learn a three-way interaction of interests and 'values' whereas previously it was bilateral. Initially at any rate, the baby will have no intention of moderating its demands for food and attention and this new factor may well throw a strain on the parents relationship. In some cases it has lead to child abuse by the father or even, comparatively rarely, by the mother.

In modern Western type societies these changes are often made more difficult first by the tendency, in the professional and middle classes at any rate, for the children to come later in life and secondly, by the smaller size of the extended family. Above all by the absence in the immediate family group of older adults (such as grandparents or elderly unmarried aunts who often in earlier days stayed at home) who could help to look after the growing children often introducing them to new 'values', sometimes providing invaluable comfort and advice, helping to smooth any difficult transitions. Nowadays it is not at all unusual for both mother and grandmother to be working away from home leaving young children to be looked after by paid help who do not usually have the same commitment to the children.

- **Children and Grandchildren**

There is another marked change which takes place when grandchildren are born, and start to mature. For until one's own children experience, in their turn, the problems of raising children they are likely to have but little understanding of the problems they themselves have caused.

- **Aging**

For adults the Biblical life span used to be taken as 'three score years and ten' which, in the Western world at any rate, was for many years, a surprisingly accurate approximation to the average age at death. In this century the position has changed substantially and it is now quite customary for many to live well beyond seventy. In fact today in the UK there are well over two thousand people aged one hundred or more and the number is likely to increase dramatically over the next twenty-five years. This means that, in the Western world, the proportion of the elderly is now rising steadily and, in the absence of some major population catastrophe, the proportion of the over sixty-fives in the UK population is likely to reach 45% by the year 2020. This involves an important change in the balance between the 'active' and the 'retired' sections of the population.

This changing age differential has already had a marked effect on socially acceptable 'values' since it emphasizes the natural gap between the young and the old. It also shifts the weight of political power for, on the whole, the older voters tend to support the status quo. Broadly speaking, as people age, they become less willing to accept changes and to adjust to new ideas (in other words to modify their 'values') while the young find it easier to alter and to adjust to what they regard as relevant and appropriate changes.

While this is broadly true there are obvious exceptions such as the now general acceptance, at least in the Western world, of young couples living together before marriage now taken for granted by both young and old (almost without comment). This follows the technical revolution in birth control but it also reflects the extent to which religion has lost its earlier power to dominate our cultural 'values'.

It is worth noting that there are other important political and international implications in this 'aging' of the Western populations because, broadly speaking, the older generations tend to be less inclined to take risks something which has, of course, a more marked effect in any true democracy where, through the free and confidential vote, individuals can usually show their support of, or objection to, any particular policy.

On the whole the dictatorships (which are still common in Third World countries no matter what the nominal form of constitution) tend to have younger expanding and therefore more aggressive populations. This is a factor which, in the longer run, is likely to have a powerful effect because it must aggravate the confrontation which all present evidence indicates must inevitably come as the wave of population (due about 2050) creates demands for basic resources such as clean water, fuel and for more living space something the existing democracies are likely to resist strongly.

- **Aging - Further**

Reverting now to the history of the individual, the age factor becomes of growing importance as time slips by. By the time age eighty is reached the individual becomes very conscious of the fact that their expectation, their likely future lifetime, is beginning to disappear seemingly at an ever increasing rate and, if there are things they wish to do, now is the time to do them. While this is not likely to affect basic 'values' it does very much influence the way priorities are assessed and determined.

Sometimes it is useful to visualize life as a form of marathon with an uncertain finishing line. Early on you need to position yourself and to do this a special effort may be necessary but, in general, there is no point in exhausting one's abilities and powers in continuous spurts. However, as the race draws to its close (and it is one of the nicer subtleties of life that mostly we never know when that will be) then the future ceases to have the same power over our imagination and our priorities change to accommodate this.

Again, as age increases, all bodily functions tend to change. To some extent this may be offset by gained experience but if zest for life is to be maintained the maximum use should be made of the experience which has been gained in order to compensate for any deterioration in one's faculties. To come to terms with these physical and mental changes (including - for many - the important sexual feature) one's objectives must be modified, dramatically in some instances, because of the psychological and social implications of those physical and mental changes.

- **Is Life a Boon?**

Sadly one of the main problems, particularly at the more advanced ages, is that many individuals begin to revert to the attitudes of early childhood concentrating on their own needs and wishes, largely to the exclusion of others. Zest for life often virtually disappears and personal interactions diminish to a marked extent. If this happens it can become a very sad time and many say they would prefer not to have to continue to struggle with a life which has 'lost its savour'. Here we are touching on one of the 'Absolutes' put forward by many forms of religion - whether it is ever 'right' to take human life and if so, in what circumstances.

- **Euthanasia & Abortion**

The taking of human life is one of the fundamental 'values' leading to the wider debate regarding euthanasia, abortion and the reintroduction in this country of the death penalty. These are matters where the strongest opinions are held and basic questions arise on whether, and to what extent, modern conditions and current generally accepted 'values' are modifying the Mosaic command 'Thou shalt not kill'.

Personally I have no doubt that, in specific circumstances (and with proper safeguards laid down by law), individuals should have the right to terminate their own life or, once again with appropriate precautions, to arrange for some loved one (even that of a child) to cease to live if life itself has become an intolerable burden or has been reduced to that of a vegetable needing a continuous and indefinite life-support system with no prospect of recovery. Again I would support the idea that, with the proper restraints and precautions, abortions should be legally approved but I recognize there are some who still consider both practices 'immoral'. This and much of the debate on artificial insemination, the proper disposal of foetuses and similar problems which are the result of modern techniques, show how we are now being confronted with issues which were unthinkable but a comparatively short time ago.

These are cultural, group and also individual 'value' matters which are growing in importance every day. Developments in medicine now enable many to survive when previously they would have died naturally, often peacefully, so that if an individual feels life has become a burden and wishes it to cease, then it would seem only 'fair' that their wishes should be respected.

This means changing one of society's basic 'values', and laws, in order that scarce medical and other resources (often desperately needed for other human purposes) can be better used than in keeping elderly people alive against their will. There are many people who are facing this problem who, if a referendum was held in the UK, would vote for properly controlled euthanasia a practice which, in tightly controlled conditions, is now legally acceptable in Holland, in the Northern Territory in Australia and has recently survived challenges in the Courts in the USA.

The belief that the preservation of life is sacrosanct IN ALL CIRCUMSTANCES seems now very questionable and it is relevant to quote the early nineteenth century advice to a doctor

> *Thou shalt not kill; but needst not strive*
> *Officiously to keep alive.*

advice which would seem equally relevant today.

- **Illness and 'Values'**

Illnesses can play an important part in forming establishing or developing 'values'. We all know that some of the more lovable people have 'values' which lead them to devote their lives to the sick and the dying and personal illness can also play an important part in toughening character - one of the outstanding examples being the American President, Franklin Roosevelt, who was transformed from a political lightweight before he had polio to one of the four dominant statesmen of the Second World War. It was a classic case of 'its not what happens to you that counts its what you do about it.' and obviously 'What you do about it' is largely determined by one's 'values'.

- **Conscience**

The individual conscience probably starts with the feeling of 'guilt' induced in young children by adults when, at that stage, most if not all of the young child's instinctive actions call forth a rebuke, or some more or less adverse comment, from the adults on whose help and protection the child depends for its survival.

Later, at a more sophisticated level, we recognize in ourselves feelings, thoughts and 'values' which conflict with family and other generally accepted communal and cultural 'values' which, in our particular group at any rate, are regarded as 'fair', 'decent', 'seemly' and therefore acceptable. Such feelings which are in accordance with our own 'values' and aimed at action to secure what we regard as our legitimate interests, are contrary to the clearly expressed interests of others so we are faced with the problem of either submerging our own interests to theirs or pursuing our own interests at their expense.

The Christian view would be that the 'right' course is to give others preference to ourselves a precept which, no doubt, should provide the guiding light in all interactions of value. One can readily accept that if a common set of 'values' based on this precept could be universally induced most, if not all, of the world's problems would disappear or at least be substantially mitigated. Unfortunately it would seem to run counter to some of the basic biological genetic factors so that, only in certain cases and for certain individuals, can it effectively be invoked as an overriding principle. But more of that later.

Conscience can then be regarded as a reaction to the inevitable conflicts between our own unique 'values' (as we visualize them whether consciously or not) and those commonly accepted by our culture or group.

If our 'values' are basically 'benevolent' we would not wish to hurt those we love but, inevitably, when conflicts of 'interests' arise we cannot always satisfy the demands of all so that in the end someone feels hurt and dissatisfied. This problem of the conflict of interests is one which occurs at minor levels all the time and we are all well versed in taking decisions, mentally balancing one claim off against another. Normally if our previous actions have provided evidence of a 'fair' and considerate attitude the problem is resolved without bitterness but in some cases, and with some people, an intense jealousy develops which can then distort a previously loving and friendly relationship.

The reality is that, on the great majority of occasions, we act without conscious thought, without weighing up the balance of interests, subconsciously judging the importance to us of the various relationships.

Chapter 3

Biological & Genetic Origins

'The child is father of the man' - Wordsworth

'Qualities' can be defined as the unique inherited potential, both mental and physical, with which each individual starts life that provides the substance from which 'values' emerge. They determine which particular 'values' are 'caught' and the differing emphasis each of us attaches to particular aspects of the spectrum of 'values' we are offered as we grow up.

It is fascinating to find that, in the notebooks which Darwin kept long before the publication of 'Origin of Species', he was speculating, as early as 1838, of thought and behaviour evolving under the constraints of 'circumstance & education' holding that antisocial behaviour (resulting from particular 'values') could be inherited. In fact he wrote:- *'Verily the faults of the fathers, corporeal & bodily are visited upon the children'* going on to conclude that accepting this 'evolutionary determinism' could transform human conduct, for a father would *'strive to improve his organization for his children's sake'* and that men *'would only marry good women & pay detailed attention to education & so put their children in the way of being happy'.*

A remarkable tribute to his 'values', but, sadly, not to his realism. And it was his fear of the impact of his ideas on his wife, and on the Establishment 'values' of the day rather than the effect of those ideas on contemporary scientific thought, which led him to defer publication for so long. When publication did take place, many of the leading Churchmen feared, rightly, that once the concept of evolution was generally accepted (which meant humanity was not directly, and specifically, created by God as the Old Testament said) the whole of their structure of Absolute Values, dependent on this myth would be invalidated.

It was Huxley who, when he became convinced of what he regarded as the indisputable logic of Darwin's case, took the fight to the Bishops and to the rest of the Establishment, a fight in which Darwin finally, and reluctantly, joined. At that time Harriet Martineau (a leading Unitarian and a close friend of the Darwin family) was arguing against any *'universal moral sense'* claiming that, among humans, *'right'* and *'wrong'* were culturally conditioned, not spiritually endowed. Darwin finally accepted that *'moral norms'* are formed by external influences and all *'vices'* and *'virtues'* must depend on their social context.

However Darwin held that all humans have some sort of morality because *'man like deer'* was a *'social animal'*. He held that some moral acts were as instinctive as the deer's cough (which warned others against danger) and had evolved from the social instincts necessary to aid the cohesion of the human ancestral troop. They were, therefore, socially useful by helping to cement relationships. Even the Christian precepts *'do unto others as yourself'* and *'love thy neighbour as thyself'* had evolved naturally out of our ancestors *'sexual, parental & social instincts'*.

By the autumn of 1838 he had thrashed out what were regarded as most of the social and moral issues with a small group of his immediate associates and had worked them into his evolutionary formula thus enormously expanding its scope. He noted - *We have emotions like revenge and anger because they benefited our ape ancestors. Our descent, then, is the root of our evil passions', 'Good' and 'Evil' are not moral absolutes so much as monkey attributes* and in even more graphic terms *'The Devil under form of Baboon is our grandfather.'*

At this time Darwin read and absorbed the implications of the sixth edition of Malthus' *'Essay on the Principle of Population'* which proved to be a seminal work for it emphasized that an identical struggle for survival took place throughout nature which became a truly creative force enabling the favoured 'sports' to survive while the others gradually disappeared. The struggle between species had already been an accepted idea among some scientists but nobody had so far suggested that there was the same type of competition going on inside each species.

It took another twenty years for the 'Origin of Species' to be printed, and the implications regarding the origin of 'values' were then appreciated by but a few. And, obviously, some of those implications have still not gained full acceptance today.

- **Law and the Mind**

In Professor Margaret Gruter's book on 'Law and the Mind' regarding the biological origin of certain `values' and of 'human law' (already referred to in Chapter 2) she records that in 1970 she became responsible for the development of a medical facility housing 150 mentally retarded individuals of all ages. She was helped by her husband (also a doctor) and her daughter (a biologist) and her experience led her to question many of the accepted ideas dealing with the human mind and abilities particularly as they related to the people she was concerned with. She became convinced that psychological explanations were inadequate to understand, and effectively to treat, the mental disabilities she faced daily.

Such explanations, and the social and chemical therapies then used, were proving inadequate so that while the 'patients' received the necessary nurture she recognized the limits of their improvement was set by the way their brain functioned. To her this emphasized the intimate relationship between brain/mind, perceived 'interests' and the individual's 'values' which virtually determined their 'behaviour'.

As Darwin had written much earlier she came to believe that any study of the concept of 'values' should be more fruitful, and was likely to prove more scientific, if it adopted a biological approach. She came to the conclusion that 'values', a product of the human mind are, initially, a by-product of the biological mechanisms which have been evolved to aid survival for both the individual and the species and that an important part of those mechanisms was the almost universal human quest for 'order' and 'equity' ('fairness').

She concluded that an understanding of evolutionary biology, as well as an appreciation of early human cultural achievements, was essential to provide a practical approach to the origin of human 'values'. She maintained that recognition of the balance, continuity and unity of these factors in the human brain was a vital step in understanding how 'values' are acquired and modified.

- **Rule Making and Rule Obeying**

Humans, the most versatile and adaptive of primates, find common ground in their need for *'order' and 'justice'* (*'fairness'* is probably a better word since 'justice' has a legalistic connotation which is probably inappropriate in the earlier stages of social grouping). The results of studies of child development, particularly in the origin and acquisition of language, emphasize the need for 'rules' and 'laws' to enable us to establish a sense of mental order on the initially chaotic-seeming world which we experience as children so that 'values', which include and must inevitably involve rule-making, rule-incorporating and rule-obeying, become an integral part of almost every 'normal' individual's development. The human brain normally favours connections over disjunction and most of us are biologically programmed to recognize and select data which appears to generate a pattern over data which calls patterns into question.

The concept that human 'values' have a biological origin does not imply that 'behaviour' is fixed since experience, particularly interaction with others, will influence and cause it to adjust and change. Research is revealing the 'plasticity' of behaviour among most species and while it emphasizes the importance of our genetic make-up it also shows the extent to which 'interaction of values' influences behaviour. It also stresses that, usually, there are constraints on that 'plasticity'.

Taken from the legal aspect, Professor Gruter pointed to the almost universal differences of treatment in divorce laws between the father and the mother over the custody of children. No matter how much the creators of custom and law might wish to treat parents equally they have to recognize the basic biological fact that, unless there is very strong and well substantiated evidence the mother is unsuitable, the presumption must be made, for young children in particular, that the mother should be the preferred parent.

Rules, 'values' and laws which are firmly based on biological reality are far more likely to be generally regarded as 'fair' (and therefore likely to gain wide acceptance) than any which ignore, or play down, such biological realities.

- **Fairness and Justice**

There would, therefore, seem to be a compelling case for a biological explanation for much of the sense of 'fairness' which leads on to a more formalized concept of 'justice'. Formal law in a culture or a community is a product of the interaction of many individual values while a personal sense of 'fairness' is the result of all the factors which have produced the individual's 'values' including the subtle one of brain chemistry. While it is evident that what one society calls 'fair' and 'just' does not apply universally yet underlying the differences are usually common biological factors and, on some important issues, there is often cross-society, cross cultural, consensus.

- **Research on the Brain**

Our biological inheritance of any kind of 'value' must come to us via the structure of the brain and research on the brain (neuro-anatomy, neurotransmitters etc.) is producing evidence on the anatomical network, the chemistry and the complex mechanisms involved. These are beginning to provide some explanation of the wide differences found between individuals whose cultural and family backgrounds are so similar that such wide differences in adult 'values' would otherwise be hard to understand. Such inherited factors would help to explain how very different concepts of 'fairness' (and the other interactive 'values') can develop side by side in different individuals exposed to much the same environment. These studies are leading to a concept of unique individual brain mechanisms from which an individual sense of 'fairness' emerges which is then modulated by the family and social environment in which the individual is brought up and lives.

Currently there is evidence that there are specific brain mechanisms which influence individuals helping them to achieve a sense of 'balance' and 'structure' in their lives. When this subtle chemistry is disturbed (as happens in the case of the illness 'fructosaemia') the resulting aberrant behaviour can cause bewilderment both to the individual and to the parents and much damage to family life.

- **Saints and Demons and the 'Normal Distribution Curve'**

Earlier it was mentioned it seems likely that individuals may well vary in respect of some aspects of their mental inheritance, as in so many physical features, according to the Normal Distribution Curve. If this is so the great majority of us fall, happily for us, in the central area of the curve enabling us readily to absorb the communally acceptable ideas of 'fairness' and 'decency'. If this concept is valid, (and I cannot cite any direct evidence) there must be at each end of the distribution, individuals who differ from the general run to such an extent that the rest of humanity regards them, on the one hand, as 'saints', and on the other, as 'demons' because their behaviour deviates so far from what is generally accepted as 'normal'.

Some of these individuals become the stuff from which the saints arise, those exceptional people who find fulfilment in self-abnegation while, at the other end of the distribution we find the other fringe those individuals who provide the human 'demons' whose 'self-centredness' remains uninfluenced and unchanged so that what they wish to do is all-important and is 'right' in their eyes irrespective of the mores of their society and the evil effect their actions will have on others.

This idea of a distribution of abilities to 'catch' commonly accepted 'values' would seem to be supported, to some extent at least, by the condition known as Asperger's Syndrome. This applies to a tiny proportion in whose mind everything is absolutely literal and immediate so that concepts, such as 'values' and interactions of 'interests' and 'values' (all of which are concerned with relating our behaviour to the likely consequences of that behaviour) are untenable.

While this suggestion regarding the distribution of differing abilities to 'catch' different 'values' is, at the moment, pure hypothesis it seems possible that at some time the human genome project (mapping and establishing our inherited genes) might reveal a pattern of causing Asperger's Syndrome. This could lead to a more general recognition of the way the ability to absorb different 'values' varies from one person to another.

- **Toleration & Limits**

For a society to function reasonably effectively, tolerance of others' 'interests' and 'values' is essential but limits must be set even to the virtue of tolerance and those limits will be established by the laws and customs arising from the culture's main philosophy, ethics and religion. This important aspect is dealt with more fully in the Chapter on Ethics, Philosophy and Religion.

- **The Evolution of Law in Ethnological Perspective**

Professor Gruter also drew attention to the way the origins of law and of social order are rooted in the behaviour of early humans and their primate ancestors. Man-made law provides a particular aspect of 'values'. Such 'laws' are ideas and commands expressed in words usually in a recorded form. These ideas and the consequent commands are developed by the mind interpreting the past for action in the present with a view to influencing the future. They are, therefore, intended to cover both known actions and events not as yet experienced. Man-made law is unique in its influence on human 'values' and therefore on human actions.

Nowadays, certainly in Western type societies, it must be adaptable to the realities of a rapidly changing technical and cultural world but inevitably it tends to lag behind the changes which are taking place so rapidly. The effectiveness of any law depends on its ability to influence and, in the ultimate, to control the 'values' of groups of individuals when the laws themselves have usually been determined by a relatively small set. The effectiveness of such laws depends, therefore, on 'legal behaviour' which implies a recognition of the benefits likely to be derived from such behaviour.

It is obvious that individuals obey, evade or ignore the law depending on how their individual 'values' interact with the 'value' concepts expressed in those laws. The 'values' embodied in the legal system which control, in whole or in part, 'legal behaviour' did not develop in a vacuum but, with other 'values', they evolved mainly over the period of `recent` human evolution which we regard as 'civilized', a period which has been put at about ten thousand years representing only about four hundred generations i.e. just a small proportion of the space of human life on the earth.

We have good reason to believe that, for long periods, our ancestors lived in groups ranging from fifty to two hundred persons and, to survive, they had to evolve common 'values' enabling them to protect and to raise children until those children reached biological and social maturity. From the earliest times mothers, or other adults, had to reassure, direct and teach infants and children to interact with one another.

Quite complex 'language' (partly spoken and partly sign/body language) had to be developed to communicate facts about the environment and in particular rules for 'sharing' had to be evolved. Early in human evolution such rules, critical for survival, had to be worked out and taught to infants and to young children. They had to be enforced by the mothers and other adults. Rule-following 'values' were intertwined with other 'values' influencing behaviour essential to survival which would be enhanced naturally by selection.

One author (Fox) writes:-

'Our ancestors were [biologically] selected for speaking, classifying and rule-making, creatures who could apply these talents to the breeding system. Whatever succeeded was built into the cortical processes. This included the intellectual and emotional apparatus'

- **Concepts of Law & Social Order**

A useful definition of 'Law' is:-

The rules of law are felt and regarded as the obligations of one person and the rights of another. They are sanctioned not by mere psychological motive but by a definite social machinery of binding force based upon mutual dependence and realized in the arrangement of reciprocal services as well as in the combination of such claims into strands of multiple relationships. The ceremonial manner which implies public control is intended to add to their binding force.

This definition stresses the difference between legal 'rules' and other 'rules' (mores) emphasizing the need for a social machinery to act as a 'binding force'.

Other primates follow rules - non-human primates contest dominance in predictable ways and seldom injure one another in the process. Humans seek, develop and elaborate rules. They evoke the symbol of justice, preach the dogma of equality before the law and, in most cases, they obey the law if their own 'values' hold the law to be 'fair'. Laws which are at cross purposes with strong biological influences (e.g. in modern times anti-abortion &/or conception laws or euthanasia) often imposed for ideological or religious reasons, tend to be short-lived or are largely disregarded.

The conflict between biologically based rules and mores and others which are of a later more socially orientated nature is emphasized in the old saying 'Everything is fair in Love and War.'

- **Natural Law**

For at least 3000 years Western philosophers and jurists have tried to construct legal systems that encouraged a reasonably predictable and peaceful social system and man-made laws were the principal tool used to achieve this end.

The earlier Greek cosmologists, Thales and Antiphon (who naturally lacked the benefit of the results of modern biological research) emphasized the difference between nature (physics) and law or convention (nomos) arguing that the varying customs and laws of each society differed from the *'rules of nature'* which everywhere must be the same. The Sophists reasoned that human laws were conventions based on self-interest and there was no natural basis while Plato and Aristotle held there was a right for *'justice'* which was *'according to nature.'*

This led to the idea of *'natural law'* in the Justinian Code which, in the middle ages, Thomas Aquinas established as the symbol of Christian justice. This egalitarian attitude stemmed from the Judaic interpretation of the Old Testament summed up in the statement *'the sanctification of each member of the community who obeys the laws of Yahweh implies an equality of all men'*.

Thus in societies with a Judaic/Christian background *'natural law'* has provided a general foundation for written or common law, the Church earlier claiming that religious law was superior to civil law.

Aquinas' concept of an unchanging *'law of nature'* which upheld the *'eternal verities'*, the ABSOLUTES, was taught well into the eighteenth century as a basic fact of life. With Darwin the modern interaction between biology and 'values' began and our view of Man ceased to be that of a special creation of God who, through Christ, the prophets and the Bible, had provided humanity with the necessary 'values' to live a *'good' life*, 'values' and principles which would provide the basis of *'right'* laws. All of which should lead to a rewarding `life after death`. And it became generally accepted that *'common law'* should be viewed as an evolving system which changed in response to the interaction between *'the deepest instincts of man'* and the effect of the new and changing conditions.

As Darwin feared, his ideas have, for many, seriously undermined the authority of many religious leaders and also the common belief that the Church's views on *'ultimate values'*, the churchmen's interpretation of the 'Absolutes', should be accepted without question. The concept of unquestioning obedience and of the acceptance of 'ex cathedra' statements by leaders, whether Pontiffs or others, has, for many if not most, lost its original compulsion.

In this century Ehrlich, a leading legal authority, put forward the concept of *'the living law'* which looked at the interaction of 'values' with the legal system - the law in action, as it worked in reality, rather than the law of the books.

- **Ethology**

This is a branch of biology based on the study of animals in their natural environment and, while some authorities have held that mankind is so different from other mammals that any deductions from the behaviour of other mammals is likely to be misleading, the more widely held view is now that, provided the study is carefully made so that the observer is not likely to distort the behaviour observed, there is much to be learned from such work. Through direct observation scientists seek to identify rules of behaviour vital to the survival and reproduction of the species. The studies concentrate on four main areas:-

- Ultimate causation - the selection factors which result in species' characteristics influencing particular behaviour

- Development function - gene inheritance, interactions with environment (including learning)

- Function - how different behaviour patterns are favoured by Natural Selection causing animals to behave in predictable ways and

- Proximate Mechanisms - factors which cause short-range behaviour change

Ethologists are now in broad agreement that genetic differences influence behaviour, that gene/environment interactions influence the degree of genetic expression and that individual capacities, and therefore behaviour, are further modified by the pattern of development and learning. If, under the final section, one were to include the factor of "acquisition of 'values'" this would seem to be a good summary of the process which normally takes place in humans.

In some species the learning period is short and, moving through different species from the most primitive mankind, the degree to which genetic inheritance contributes to specific behaviours would seem to decline. It would therefore seem that if 'imprinting' does occur in humans, in many instances it is largely reversible or subject to modification.

For instance we know that certain diseases (such as depression, schizophrenia and personality problems including antisocial and hysterical behaviour as well as some forms of alcoholism) are influenced by genetic factors but this is not a deterministic sentence since ethology provides equally convincing evidence that individual behaviour is modifiable by experience and by learning. There are of course limits even to human abilities to modify genetic inheritance and much study in this area is directed to establishing these limits.

For group mores/values (and any legal system based on them) to be acceptable they must rely on shaping individual 'values' within the limits of human plasticity achievable by the broad majority. Anthropological studies have shown that in any society a social mechanism develops which, to a certain extent, allows and sanctions deviant behaviour. This is an important distinction which separates legal behaviour among humans from the rule-following among primates.

The concept of a 'Living Law' guiding the interaction of 'values' which influence if not control individual and group behaviour continues into technological societies and the most effective formal law would be one which conforms reasonably well with that 'Living Law' its main function being to ease the flow of events, to constrain excesses and, when necessary, to restore balance. Successful legislation is dependent on a recognition of general 'values' and mindful of biological influences on the individual's 'values'.

• The Relevance of Ethology

Recent findings by molecular scientists emphasize the close link in the genetic endowment of apes and humans and biological techniques have now placed the chimpanzees and the gorillas as closest to humans. Such analyses are important in three ways: -

- Firstly they are informative regarding the importance of genetic contributions to behaviour. Thus apes and humans behave differently, in part because of different genetic endowment, yet both have developed complex communication systems. Apes cannot use complex verbal language because the formation of their throats (a genetic factor) makes it impossible to form words. However they are capable of dealing with complex situations and of using non-verbal messages to give directions, specify locations and clarify relationships.

- Secondly such findings give an indication of the complexity of physiological/anatomical mechanisms affecting behaviour and therefore of the underlying 'values'.

- Thirdly the findings have an importance for law - to what extent is it realistic for laws to require individuals to carry out, or to refrain from, actions which are contrary to biological inheritance? Can (or should) law provide for continuous adaptive change in channelling human behaviour faced with the major changes in our environment which are now occurring at an accelerating pace?

Summing up it seems highly probable that human 'values' (and therefore human behaviour influenced and/or controlled by those 'values') are shaped by a combination of the following factors:-

- 1. Genetic predispositions.

- 2. Development experience leading to learning.

- 3. Environmental factors including social demands and options.

Certain functions such as actions to acquire resources or to succeed in sexual encounters are likely to be more resistant to change by regulation than less fundamentally biologically based drives. Deviance from the 'values' (and any law) is more likely when the required 'norm' runs counter to a fundamental 'biological drive'. Therefore the effectiveness of any 'value', custom or law is likely to be broadly proportional to the extent that the required behaviour complements or contravenes any such 'biological drive'. Examples which we are most conscious of arise most frequently in the areas of sexuality, reproduction and aggression.

Some 'values' and laws seek to encourage, some to discourage, reproduction. Others to encourage pair-bonding between the opposite sexes and to discourage it between the same sex. Again this is an area of substantial change certainly over the last twenty-five years in Western societies. Many other 'values' and laws in all societies seek to help to perpetuate the family while others seek to curb aggressive behaviour and to protect group members particularly the young, the aged and the handicapped. In some conditions 'values' and laws will actually encourage aggression e.g. in protection of one's life, family and, in some areas, one's property. In the case of what is considered to be *'the national interests'* even murder, is not only tolerated but actually encouraged and required although it is, naturally enough, not labelled with that name.

These multiple relationships between 'values' may seem paradoxical but are really only the surface manifestation of the infrastructure where biology and 'values' interface. They are 'values' we learn unconsciously and usually without critical thought as we 'grow up'. It should be noted that the relationship between 'values', the law and behaviour is not simple and direct. Criminal laws are meant to punish the guilty, to be a deterrent helping to protect the innocent and, where practicable, helping to restore social order by rehabilitating the offender.

Human 'values', laws and mores passed down to us from preceding generations are deeply rooted in the biology of early humans and are themselves unconsciously influenced by the 'rules' similar to those which are observed to exist in non-human primates. This applies to the 'values' and laws of indigenous traditional societies but, to a lesser extent, also to the more sophisticated and complex 'values' found in more technically advanced societies. Laws change as 'values' change and the timing and sequence of these changes, whether the law leads or follows, can have a significant influence on the effectiveness of the laws themselves.

- **Biological Studies and the Law**

Studies of non-human primate behaviour can thus provide useful insights into the way human 'values' develop and, therefore, into our own probable behaviour provided the analysis is conducted in a balanced way. It is important here to stress that 'biology' here means the study of 'life' whereas in medicine and philosophy the word more often has the connotation of physiology and genetics.

It is now generally accepted that the evolution of species operates by the natural selection of 'behaviours' which are associated with different patterns of survival and reproduction as conditions change. Basically there are two ways successful behaviour patterns can be transmitted one is by changes in genetic 'information' and the other is by experience and learning and here again the capacity to learn has, itself, to be transmitted.

In the case of humans some things are learned more readily than others e.g. walking upright, avoiding obstacles, speaking and counting. Equally there are constraints on behaviour and one of the functions of man-made law is to strengthen the helpful constraints. More detailed investigation has shown that there are such things as neuro-transmitters, receptor sites and ion channels which are involved in such factors as developing affectional bonds and also in competitive behaviour.

In the absence of extreme isolation (or many changes in very early childhood) predisposed behaviour contributes significantly to the adult's character as is shown by similarities in human behaviour in widely different cultures and environments.

- **Guidelines**

Biologists use guidelines for extrapolating from non-human to human behaviour. The first deals with analogies and homologies. Analogy refers to cross-species similarities (the mother-infant bond seen in non-human primates such as whales and birds as well as in humans which serves the same purpose providing the young with the essential protection and nutrition) while homology refers to cross-species similarity in terms of evolutionary history. Functional similarity may or may not be present (the wings of birds and human arms are homologous but serve very different purposes). The analogous relationships are usually more informative as they illustrate the different ways similar species have solved the same environmental problem.

The second guideline concerns the difference between ultimate and proximate explanations of behaviour. Ultimate explanations deal with why certain behaviours were likely to be selected during evolution while proximate explanations deal with the details of current behaviour e.g. what neurotransmitter changes occur when frightened by a snake. Proximate mechanisms may well have ultimate causes but the investigative focus is on their short-term operation.

There is a further factor, that of probability. If a certain behaviour is observed only rarely the statistical basis is too small to be reliable. Again it must be stressed that the behaviour of captive animals is unlikely to be a good guide to behaviour in more natural surroundings. It is therefore essential to be sceptical and treat any observations and deductions in this area with caution.

- **Kin Selection**

There are some cross-species similarities in anatomy, physiology, behaviour and, in some instances, the ability to learn. Some of the findings on animal behaviour are reflected in human 'values' and therefore in the law. Studies of altruism provide a good example. Animals can behave in a way that, to us, appears 'altruistic' and not obviously directly in accordance with their self-interest. But it has been pointed out that helping one's kin helps the survival of some of one's own genetic material which has led to the development of the 'kin-selection' theory and of the concept of 'reciprocal altruism'.

The 'kin selection' concept is based on the likelihood of an inherited preference for the children of the closest relative and then of siblings, (such as nieces who are likely to reproduce) because *'I am investing in myself'*. There is evidence indicating that many non-human primates protect their own offspring and the offspring of siblings in preference to others. While, in one way, such 'self-investment' may well help one's genetic material to survive it can also lead to overprotection and thus a weakening of the individual which would tend to have the opposite effect in some circumstances.

In the legal area the 'kin selection' factor is clearly accepted in our inheritance laws where favourable treatment of family is customary and special rules for giving to kin are almost universal, family bonds being recognized as a vital factor in maintaining group and social order. Various forms of 'nepotism' are part of our accepted 'values' for we raise our children and often deprive ourselves not only to give them a 'better' education but we are also often willing to do this for our grandchildren as well.

Family bonds play an important part in maintaining group and social order which are assisted by hierarchical relationships within the group. An adult who is head of a family not only assumes various roles (mother, provider, companion etc.) but also assigns other roles to other family members according to their age, sex and perceived abilities. *'From each according to their ability, to each according to their need'* is a good family rule provided the person determining the 'ability' and the 'need' can be relied upon to be 'fair'. One consequence of this 'role-assignment' is the encouragement of 'values' which modify pure self-centredness and encourage altruistic action such as family members helping and giving succour to kin who are ill or infirm.

Among groups of non-kin the operation of an extended form of 'reciprocal altruism' leads to cooperative behaviour of a more social kind. From this come interdependent groups of related and non-related individuals and therefore the need to develop 'group-relevant' rules which become ever more important as the size of the group grows and the degree and complexity of interdependence increases. Thus, particularly in modern Westernized societies, altruistic traits associated with the realization, and acceptance, of the fact that one must now depend on non-kin for help and support encourages a drive to seek a place within a structured group. All this helps rule-making and rule-following 'values'.

At some stage of human development the subconscious recognition and acceptance of such interdependent 'values' would have enabled the shift from a hunter-gatherer type of social organization to a lifestyle based on agriculture which was the beginning of civilization as we know it. It is exemplified in the biblical story of Cain and Abel and much of the shift probably occurred only about 400 generations ago!

Another major jump came with the industrial revolution when groups became so large, and for many the kinship factor so diluted, that community forms of social cooperation, particularly within urban areas, became essential if the fabric was to hold together. It is this lack of social cohesion through the inevitable breakdown of family interdependence and authority which is one of the major factors in the inner-city troubles now being experienced in so many parts of the world. It would seem that our ability to interact with others' 'values' tends to breakdown as population pressure increases, something which has also been observed in the animal world.

To what extent it is practicable to restore kin-related 'values' and, therefore, the acceptance of family and other authority, is for us a major question which has not yet been satisfactorily resolved. It is linked to the common demand for 'rights' and the concurrent refusal, by many of the young in the West to recognize and accept responsibilities takes us back to the dichotomy between the Greco/Roman and the Eastern cultures Sir James Frazer emphasized in The Golden Bough.

The question of survival of ourselves, our kin and therefore of our 'values' has been raised to a higher level by the new techniques for long-distance mutual destruction calling into place interactions (of 'values') on a worldwide scale to an extent which would have been unthinkable one or two generations ago. Since it seems impracticable to alter, sufficiently quickly, the wide diversity of interests and 'values' held with such conviction by many national, religious and cultural groups there is a real danger that persuasion, argument and diplomacy will prove to be inadequate. If this proves to be so then some form of re-colonization may well become essential if our form of civilization is to survive.

- **Mother-Infant Bonding**

The long period of primate-young dependency on their mothers is a common factor which still persists although it may be lessening in some parts of Western type societies. The focus of the family is on procreation and the care of the young until they reach reproductive age at least. Observations of non-human primates indicate that a mother and an infant (or in some cases any adult and an infant) when in close bodily contact tend to be treated as a unit usually inhibiting aggression. Examples have been recorded of young male baboons seizing an infant to avert aggression by stronger animals.

- **Bonds - Families & Non-relatives**

In typical non-human primate families, aunts and juvenile sisters and brothers tend to protect their younger siblings from attacks or abuse by non-kin. Sometimes males protect not only their own offspring but also the offspring of others. And grandmothers will protect grand-offspring. Infants object to weaning, siblings engage in competitive behaviour to attract the attention of parents so that kin-bonds extend way beyond the mother-infant relationship thus providing a basis for group order, cross-animal obligations and, to some extent, predictable interactions. Non-kin reciprocal relationships such as grooming have frequently been observed. Animals reconcile after fights, give general warnings of the approach of a predator and during periods of low food supply tend to reduce their own food intake. At the same time there is plenty of evidence of self-interest expressed through hierarchies and high-status males and their females usually have priority access to preferred foods, sleeping places and quite often require grooming by 'inferior' animals.

Thus while there are evolved tendencies making for pair-bonding, group cohesiveness and cooperation, there is, alongside those tendencies, ample evidence of selfish, self-serving and even exploitive behaviour but, for non-human primates, there is no evidence so far of any mechanism corresponding to the body of 'values' exemplified by the human legal system.

In human societies the bonds which encourage cohesiveness (thus helping the survival of that particular gene-bank) are so strongly part of our nature, and so essential to the everyday 'interaction of values', that at an early age children accept these bonds as an essential part of learning how to behave. It is true that mothers sometimes desert their babies, there are cases of infanticide, children run away from home and live 'wild' and kin murder one another (in fact most murders occur within the family!) but basic 'values' exist for most individuals influencing and constraining behaviour. The extent to which an individual's 'values' determine his/her actions in seeking their 'interests' is modified, all the time, by the interaction of those 'values' with the others with whom they are in contact directly or indirectly.

- **Family Law**

It is interesting to consider how these deep-rooted 'values' are translated into 'family law'. First, regardless of cultural differences and environmental changes, the mother-infant bond persists among nearly all mammals and, where there is pair-bonding, the family unit usually includes an adult male. While the forms and structures of family units differ in human societies the plasticity of human 'values' (and therefore of behaviour) is far greater, resulting in a much wider variety in the forms of bonding such as the homosexual relationships found (and nowadays often applauded) in so many different societies from the East to the West.

Environmental and cultural factors are crucial in determining which form of family structure generally prevails and any legal efforts to change meet with increasing resistance and generally prove unsuccessful such as the attempts in Muslim countries to restrict or to eliminate polygamy.

Most of the 'values' derived from the biological family and bonding are already implicit in existing legal systems in very different parts of the world and in very different cultures. In virtually all, a mother's obligation to her child is taken for granted and the law deals, in some cultures harshly, with a mother who is not carrying out her 'duties' or is maltreating a child. Again in many societies somewhat similar rules apply to a father's responsibility for his young offspring.

Laws do not generally impose heavy obligations on adult siblings although there may well be strong social constraints on rejecting the claims of a brother or sister in need. Individuals who reject or ignore such 'values' can find themselves socially ostracized. The great majority of both mothers and fathers will seek to protect their children even to the extent of risking and, in the ultimate, sacrificing their own lives if that is essential. If basic resources are scarce individuals will prefer their kin to others and this can well lead to violence even to murder. It is in such areas that the law (if it is being effectively enforced) must intervene to make peaceful coexistence practicable.

Finally, family structure is based on the functions allocated to, or adopted by, different members of the family. There is a head of the family and other members assume complementary roles. Today spouses may share the dominant role each striving to sustain their supremacy in certain areas of decision taking. Yet almost universally family structure shows social order in a hierarchical or dominance pattern and this occurs wherever humanity forms any type of group such as parliaments, clubs or athletic teams.

- **Group Order & Fairness**

All species, and Homo sapiens in particular, are characterized by wide differences in genetic patterns. Sexual reproduction results in a continual mixing of genetic material so the resulting individuals differ in their capacity to make 'rules, to understand them and to translate them into their 'values'. In humanity there has obviously been a natural selection favouring genes leading to 'values' which have helped us to cope with our environment more successfully than, so far, has happened with other species. Those 'values' have permitted and, indeed, encouraged the widely different types of behaviour enabling us to cope successfully with climatic conditions varying from the Poles to the Sahara and from the depths of the Ocean to the Moon.

As a result we continue to be strongly predisposed to 'values' leading to behaviour which, while it is self-interested, does permit and, indeed in the right circumstances, encourages a degree of altruism. The 'right' mix must be a matter of chance depending on a process of trial and error which, given the rapidly changing environment created by modern science, scarcely gives the evolutionary process sufficient time to operate on us effectively.

A key factor in the development of 'values' encouraging interaction with non-kin is the development of means of transmitting information regarding attitudes and intentions - the natural hesitancy many people feel over going into new social settings is because of the inability to anticipate others' 'values' and behaviour - specifically whether they will 'attack' or not. If strangers, by facial or other means, indicate whether they are friendly or not this helps us to assess their likely intrinsic 'values' (to us) and makes it easier to predict their behaviour.

The development of capacities to transmit and interpret information regarding 'values' must have been associated with the human brain's increasing capacity to process more complex information thus helping the individual to make a better assessment of the likely consequences of particular actions and so to incorporate living and survival 'strategies' into their own 'values'. Thus the growing ability to formulate 'rules' and, at a much later stage, to 'enact' enforceable laws was gradually introduced into the biological inheritance and thus, for most of us, became part of our 'values'.

The rules embodied in the 'values' had to be such that the members of the group could readily understand and accept them and they had, therefore, broadly to follow the biological 'facts' already established in pre-hominoid development. For such 'values' and rules to be effective the rules would have to be specific and the social consequences of failing to comply, clear-cut. One is reminded of the Ten Commandments which, derived as they must surely have been from the sojourn of the Jews in Egypt, provided the basic laws for the Jewish wanderers during their time in the Wilderness. Simple and direct Commandments well suited to the circumstances and their environment at the time.

Our children learn the rules of any game (and the concept of 'fair-play') mostly from their siblings, they imitate older siblings and adults. People move to different places and different jobs all involving different concepts and 'values'. In some cases they have to cope with widely different cultures and to survive in such cases they have to learn to interact with widely different 'values'. They have also to recognize that in these areas 'right' and 'wrong' can have very different meanings from the ones they have been accustomed to. It can be a hard lesson to learn and some people find any such transition intolerable; these are the individuals who have to go back to their original environment in order to live comfortably.

• The Role of Law

The ability to formulate and live by 'values' embodying rules had a significant effect on human development since such 'values' and rules contributed to the growth of social cultures rich in symbolic content. The adaptability of individuals and groups is influenced by traditions of legal behaviour inherent in cultural behaviour; law and culture interacting in a dynamic way. An American writer pointed out that:-

'(Most) Americans...seem willing to pay...taxes, they evade some but within acceptable limits. On the other hand no-one obeys adultery laws simply because they are laws... State intervention in private sexual behaviour is culturally disapproved.'

Law is therefore not a set of formalized rules which people obey blindly but rather law is the formalization of generally acceptable 'values' about which most people agree and have therefore already absorbed them into their existing individual values. It is a good example of 'interaction of values' in the wider sense of the words.

As language was developed there came the capacity to believe in the supernatural so that associating law with this other factor (and the trappings of a British law court are intended to enhance this) introduced the feeling of 'guilt' if a commonly accepted law was broken.

Rules and laws are therefore reflective of social conditions, social options and expectations and are reflected in both common and individual 'values'. Broadly, legal systems reflect the facts making special provisions for minors. They also require special qualifications for those who operate the legal system and for those who are required to make decisions affecting the members of the group.

- **The Sense of Justice**

This can be described as an individual's feeling (reflecting their 'values') regarding the 'fairness' of an event or of an attitude, or the emotional reaction to behaviour regarded to be 'unjust'. This may have evolved as one of the traits helping human adaptation. It is apparent in the sense of 'equity' which helps to determine group interaction and strongly influences the extent to which individuals comply with, evade, ignore or actively disobey a particular law or conform with a particular system. This is not a fixed 'value' but one which changes with circumstances. What individuals do is influenced by their own sense of 'fairness' which is derived from their own set of 'values' interacting with the communal sense of 'justice' or 'fairness'. This is a complex matter because peoples' ideas are embodied in, and their 'values' are influenced by, the 'values' of, the many different groups in which they participate - families, religious, professional and trade, social, national etc. groups which will have different, and sometimes contradictory, group 'values' so that resolving the issue can sometimes involve serious conflicts of 'conscience'.

- **'Acceptable' Behaviour**

When individuals make value judgments on 'acceptable' behaviour (even if the behaviour is based on expediency or, in the ultimate, survival) such judgments can coalesce into commonly accepted concepts of 'right' or 'wrong'. Each member of the group has to adjust his or her 'values' to the joint 'values' of the group or face ostracism or rejection. Thus age and sex, economic factors and past experience all influence an individual's 'values'. The type of family (and its structure) in which a person grew up, the bonds and attachments developed during their early years together with the hierarchical structures and the way the individual's personal 'values' match the group 'values' all play their part in the way each one decides that justice (reasonable fairness) has prevailed.

To sum up, a person's sense of justice/fairness which is an important part of their 'values' is a complex product of innate mechanisms reacting to the particular circumstances and interacting with the 'values' of the others in their various groups. To put it in simpler language an individual has to learn how to wear different 'hats' at different times and in different circumstances - the 'hats' representing various aspects of an individual's basic 'values' evoked by the specific circumstances which need to be taken into account at a particular time in those particular circumstances.

- **Rights & Responsibilities**

Different, and sometimes very strong, emotions arise when actual behaviour does not match the expected behaviour, when the balance in a group is threatened, when someone has not been 'repaid' for helping another. Restoration of the sense of balance evokes a feeling of wellbeing in the individuals concerned. In this context 'pattern matching' becomes an essential part of the law.

- **Sexuality & the Law**

This is the area where individual and group 'values' can most obviously and dramatically differ and it is worthwhile considering the interactions here. Sexuality has three basic biological functions, pair bonding, the exchange of genetic material in procreation and brood-tending which all represent vital elements in social behaviour. With humans the majority of cultures have established explicit, or implicit, rules derived from their common 'values' for each of these functions.

Dealing first with the 'values' influencing sexual behaviour which are themselves influenced by laws dealing with family relationships, (but not those relating to 'criminal' acts which society rules to be unnatural, perverse or violent such as incest or rape). It is clear that family law has its roots in biology modified by cultural factors, the biological 'facts' being interpreted differently in different cultures and given different meanings and different 'weights' according to the prevailing philosophical, religious and ideological precepts modified according to the practical options.

For example polygamy is acceptable under Islamic law and is widely practiced among some 800 million Muslims whereas Western type jurisprudence generally treats bigamy as a crime even for people such as Mormons whose religious beliefs encourage it. Degrees of enforcement vary widely because people disregard laws dealing with sexuality more than any other type of law.

- **Pair-bonding & Marriage**

In most human societies pair-bonds are formalized in some form of ceremony which usually entails a form of legal sanction dealing primarily with the results of sexual behaviour and not specifically with the sexual behaviour itself. In some cultures such as the Hindu and the Muslim, pair-bonding is based on the exchange of women in arranged marriages. In industrialized and technological societies (particularly if women can and do earn there own living) an arranged marriage of that kind is unlikely but the choice of partner is influenced by the early induction of 'values' regarding marital roles, family approval or disapproval and the influence of peers combined with motivation based on economic considerations. Whether the male is likely to become 'a good provider' is still very important but we have not yet reached the state where the reverse is true although the attractions of a rich wife have been a notable feature at most times and at all levels of society!

Pair-bonding in terms of couples living together has, in Western type cultures, become far more common arising from the improved techniques reducing the likelihood of unwanted conception and because of the availability in many areas of vasectomy and easy, inexpensive, abortions. This is a further example of how our improved technique modifies normal biological processes which, until quite recently, were regarded as immutable factors in creating basic human 'values'.

The changes, not only in techniques controlling unwanted conception, but also in the ability of young women to be self-supporting and economically independent are making their mark in previously strongly developed family 'values' and for a daughter to be 'living with' a young man whom she may or may not marry is now acceptable by many. It can still cause problems, even murder in at least one Islamic family living in the United Kingdom where the daughter had adopted the current Western 'value' from her peers but where the father was still imbued with earlier Islamic concepts.

In more recent times, in pair-bonding in Western type societies, popular stress has been on sexual attraction (embodied in the word 'romantic') with its presumed importance for marital and pair-bonding happiness. Emphasis on this aspect has led, in many cases, to temporary pair-bonding which fails later because of differences in other 'values' particularly when one party, or both, fail to recognize and to accept the need for the tolerance and 'interaction of values' crucial for any relationship to fulfil its purpose satisfactorily.

Any purely sexual relationship ignores the importance in marriage and pair-bonding of the creation of new links among persons and families as a basis of mutual protection and help, for the transmission of genes and the care of children (if there are to be children) and as a necessary factor in helping to produce lasting and satisfying relationships. The 'values' facilitating 'pair-bonding' are multiple, complex and often triggered by hormonal changes. They are undoubtedly influenced by interaction, by seasonal changes and modulated by maturational stages. They can give a zest for life in one of its most memorable forms which, in the best circumstances, can continue until old age.

- **The Action Chain**

When the actions of one partner become the obligations of another an 'action chain' is formed. Each partner by interacting with the 'values' of the other usually produces more or less predictable behaviour patterns. Predictability not only facilitates reciprocal behaviour among group members but it also helps to create a balance among them by helping to satisfy justifiable expectations which, among humans, usually take the form of claims or rights indicating some degree of obligation for others.

One of the basic sexual differences between humanity and other mammals is the almost continuous sexual receptivity of the human female which helps to encourage more lasting close relationships between human sexual partners and, as has already been noted, in many Western type societies the motivation for sex and the pleasure, and relief from tension, associated with it, no longer need be associated with the likelihood of, and therefore the responsibility for, procreation.

While, in most complex human societies, the pair-bond and the different functions of sexual behaviour have been regulated by marital law or custom for many generations, this is hardly significant on an evolutionary time-scale. Nevertheless, today, in Western and many other societies, not only marriage but also many other aspects of the 'values' involved in pair-bonding are subject to legal regulation dealing very largely with the results of the frequent breakdown of pair-bonding, in the form of divorce if a marriage ceremony has taken place, or separation if it has not. Such laws concentrate mainly on the social results of the breakdown.

Other laws deal with adultery, the unwanted results of premarital sex, incest, rape, prostitution and sexual offences against minors. Nowhere else is legislation and adjudication so difficult and so controversial nor are violations of the law so incompletely reported. Obviously such laws are only likely to be effective where they conform reasonably with the 'values' influencing the behaviour they are intended to control. Therefore it is important to set out to induce 'values' which lead to interaction of pair-bonding with other biological functions and which encourage within-group interactions helping to link the members in kinship groups. Also by encouraging the stabilizing effect of predictable behaviour-chains, developing cooperation and the division of labour, and above all by encouraging altruism a vital 'value' in providing the essential social cement.

• Artificial Insemination, Incest & Genetic Exchange

Until quite recently the exchange of genetic material among humans was solely a function of sexuality and there have been widespread customs, rules and laws discouraging incest in most cultures and communities. With modern methods of artificial fertilization (and now the ability to freeze and keep sperm almost indefinitely) this has changed dramatically creating a variety of conflicts among the 'values' derived or influenced by the supporters of different religions and ideologies. These changes have given rise to new terms in our language for it is now realistic to talk of biological parent, genetic parent, social parent, birth mother, adoptive parent, sperm donor and even sperm seller.

New 'values' are being created applying to offspring's rights, and relationships are being created which were unthinkable only a decade or so ago, so that the impact of these changes in biological relationships has yet to be translated fully into commonly accepted 'values', rules, customs and laws. At the moment only a tiny proportion of Western populations is affected but the implications will inevitably spread and could well influence many existing 'values' in other more conventional spheres.

The exchange of genetic material is the cornerstone of human evolution and until now sexuality has been the key factor in determining how that exchange was effected. The full implications of the ability to select sperm and to clone have not yet been understood or realized and, for example, the very need for a male parent at all is being brought into question. George Orwell may have been premature by dating his story in 1984 but who would be rash enough today to forecast what the picture will be in 2084?

Genetic exchanges tend to widen the variety and variability of the individuals in the succeeding generations and, within certain limits, this tends to produce some variants which will be able to cope better with changes in the environment (in its widest sense). Species tend to separate into specialists and generalists, the first thriving if the existing conditions suit them while the generalists do better if conditions change. Given mankind's now amazing control over our environment it seems likely that the generalist variations are likely to survive in the longer run although, temporarily, the specialists who can cope better with the technological changes may seem to win the day. While the longer term is of importance to the survival of humanity we, as individuals, are mostly concerned with ourselves, our children and our grandchildren. Nowadays there are but few who set out to create a family dynasty.

The genetic results of inbreeding show normally in an increase in birth defects although they may well emerge later rather than earlier. In most human societies incest is barred but persists particularly in the form of sibling sexuality. However this tends to decrease before sexual maturity so that unwanted pregnancies from this cause seem to be comparatively rare. It is an area where 'values' derived from the adults forming part of the family group are obviously vital.

There have been cultures of dynastic incest in Ancient Egypt, Peru during the Inca period and in Hawaii but for the generality of individuals the prohibition held good even though the genetic concepts justifying it were not established scientifically until the late nineteenth century. The literature on kin-selection theory seems to indicate that the best seeding partners are something like second cousins who should have a small percentage of replicate genes. Many of the customs relating to marriage such as knowing the potential partner and their family would seem to have a genetic basis.

Only relatively recently in mankind's history has the possibility of an extreme mixture of genetic material become possible, or likely, with the development of cheap and rapid transport. From the earliest human times there have been waves of invaders and women and slaves have been taken, thus leading to wider genetic interchanges but, in most cultures, there have nearly always been customs, 'values' and rules reducing the extent of the potential interchange. Good examples are to be found in the Hindu caste system and in the widespread 'colour bars' which, it interesting to note, operate in India as well as in other more obvious countries. Different customs and different 'values' associated with different cultures and different creeds all provide hidden barriers to a free genetic exchange.

- **Procreation**

In most cultures and human societies (though not all) the relationship between sexual relationships and pregnancy has been known and accepted for many generations, sufficiently long for human 'values' in most cultures to be profoundly influenced, so that biology, custom, tradition, religious ideas have coalesced into 'values' and have then been consolidated into laws.

The part that sexual strategies play in creating 'values' which influence behaviour in this sphere is demonstrated by the fact that, in at least some areas in the Western world, an appreciable proportion of children have 'social' fathers who are not their biological father, the 'social' father not necessarily being aware of the fact. This has been proved by extensive blood-group testing designed to provide other information. Again resource predictability (being a 'good provider') is an important factor in a woman choosing a 'social' mate although with the growing self-supporting abilities of many women in modern Western societies this is becoming a less important factor.

In theory the best male strategy for ensuring the survival of his genetic complement would be to father as many children as possible by different mothers. In practice modern 'values' severely restrict this drive although there was the recent case of the doctor running the fertility clinic who, surreptitiously, 'donated' his sperm to many of his female patients who wanted to become pregnant. The response of many males and females to these conflicting strategies usually takes the form of jealous and possessive behaviour the male reluctant to support the offspring of another male and the female resenting any diversion of resources from her and her children.

- **The Legal Concept of Marriage**

The development of the legal concept of marriage and the wide range of laws dealing with the responsibility for caring for offspring (supplemented nowadays by State action) have contributed to the stability of the marriage and pair-bonds and, on balance, provided protection for both the children and, to some extent, for the parents. The part which religion played in creating and protecting family 'values' was originally major but it has declined dramatically with the growth of techniques largely enabling unwanted pregnancies to be avoided. The 'values' which the main Christian/Judaic concepts encourage followed the line that the major purpose of marriage and sex was reproduction in conditions which provided proper protection for the children.

Given the immense problems which the uncontrolled explosion of the world population in some areas is now causing (problems which are likely to be accentuated in the foreseeable future) current 'values' in this area may well need some basic rethinking. In the Western societies wherever individuals are influenced by Roman Catholicism, there is little immediate likelihood of the official line changing but there has been a marked alteration in 'unofficial' views which, it now seems possible, may well pervade more orthodox thinking as the Church continues to lose its power to influence and control the 'values' of its members.

Quite apart from those parts of the world influenced by Roman Catholic 'values' there are still other rapidly increasing populations which will have to be controlled if something like an inevitable disaster is to be avoided. While the rate of increase in world population seems likely to slow this is largely because, in the Western world, the increase has virtually stopped (in some areas the populations may even start to decline) while in India and the Pacific rim populations continue to expand. This must result in due course in tensions likely to upset the present fragile balances of power and it seems likely that, in time, there will be an unstoppable drive by expanding populations to take over the relatively empty areas in Australia and elsewhere.

- **Sexual Equality**

Turning to another aspect of family 'values' - whatever the drive may be for women to achieve equality with men the biological urge for many women to have, and to rear, children will mean that the ability to compete fully in the market place is likely to be limited so that it is useful to consider the relationship between birth control, abortion and the 'values' influencing the choice between them. In the USSR where birth control is poor the abortion rate is said to be the highest in the world and traditional 'values' have, it would seem, materially changed in part by the active discouragement by the State of any religious influence. It is still too early to say what the disintegration of the USSR may mean in this area but it is unlikely that the more traditional 'values' will ever regain their previous hold.

- **Summing Up**

The biological facts as they exist in terms of today's knowledge and techniques for controlling pregnancies and births can provide useful indications about 'values' which can help to influence family structure and 'interactions of values' within society but they do not and cannot provide foolproof guides. It is reasonable to believe that most children brought up in two-parent families are likely to acquire 'values' which will enable them to cope better with the ever-changing complexities of a modern technological society but, given the rate of change, it seems unlikely that our concepts of the 'best' values for this purpose will necessarily prove 'right' in the actual experience of our children.

Chapter 4

Schooling & Education

*Education has for its object the formation of Character -
Herbert Spencer*

In his book entitled 'Understanding Human Nature' Alfred Adler, the noted early psychologist, wrote in the 1920s:-

'In the course of our formal education we acquire very little knowledge of human nature and much of what we learn is incorrect because contemporary education is still unsuited to give us valid knowledge of the human mind. Every child is left to evaluate his experiences for himself and to take care of his own personal development outside the classroom. There is no tradition for the acquisition of a true knowledge of the human psyche.'

Judging by the way that in much of Western education teaching the 'humanities' has lost ground to the 'hard' sciences this comment seems as valid today as it was over seventy years ago. This may well be the main reason why more and more are turning to Eastern philosophies such as Buddhism, or the derivations of Hinduism, which emphasize the importance of human relationships and the need for humanistic 'values', seeking more satisfying answers to the fundamental questions, looking for the purpose of life on this planet in the hope of finding more fulfilment.

This view of the realities, this emphasis on the importance of interactions with others, is something which we in the West seem nowadays largely to ignore attaching far greater importance to the amazing and rapidly increasing control over our environment derived from the intelligent use of the Scientific Method in tackling our immediate more technical problems.

Today many of our pioneering thinkers are (in my view unrealistically) far more concerned with humanity's effect on the physical environment than they are on the complementary problem, on the potentially disastrous human interactions. Surely the reality is, that with the spread of nuclear and other weapons of mass destruction, we are far more likely to be endangered by others than we are from the longer term effects of our sometimes ill-considered exploitation of our physical environment. We must all be conscious of the daily proof of 'Man's inhumanity to Man' throughout the World while the evil effects of our mishandling of the Earth's resources provide, I suggest, much less cause for immediate concern.

As a sad illustration of the changing pattern of British education one can record that, when an enquiry was made some time ago at one of the leading London schools (which traditionally used to give a balanced attention to the humanities) the enquiry revealed that only two members of the sixth form were taking Greek (the discipline which used to provide much of the background to Western philosophical thinking) while the ten who wished to study philosophy had to rely on the residual amount of the teaching resources available at the senior level after the call for other subjects had been satisfied. This indicates that providing a balanced view of the purpose of life, surely a vital aspect of everyone's general education, is now largely being discarded, losing rather than gaining ground since Adler made his comments nearly three generations ago.

• Education & 'Values'

In each group it must be the adults who, while providing the children in their earliest years with the vital nurture and protection the children need, help to instil the initial basic 'values' either by example, or by word of mouth accompanied by the appropriate body language. The first stage must be when children are ready to understand, and react to, 'good!' and 'bad!' These must be the earliest 'value' judgements they recognize and this process continues until, in most civilised communities, they start at some form of school. Then they have to learn to interact more generally, and more specifically, with their peers many of whom come from different family backgrounds often with materially different family 'values'.

This exposure to children with differing 'values' is part of the informal education they get at school where most children absorb (catch) much of their earliest 'values' from those teachers they respect and like and from those of their peers they most wish to emulate.

• Religious Education

Formal education in 'values' has usually come under the heading of 'Religious Education' and in earlier times the substance was largely determined by the Church authorities who had the power to decide what was 'right' and 'wrong' for the whole community. At that stage children had clear expectations of the consequences of any contravention and on detection the resulting punishment would be backed by most parents or other adults having authority over the children. In those days most teachers were generally esteemed.

The Second World War years had a major effect especially as the father, and sometimes the mother as well, was involved in the Services or some other form of war work so that many children were left to the care of adults who did not have the same bonding with them. After the war when the family units were re-established it was a time when there was generally a more liberal philosophy and with the weakening authority of the Church the clear-cut values it promulgated lost their force.

This led to the 'swinging sixties' influencing those in authority in education, which became experimental leading to a difficult period for any believer in traditional teaching and a structured approach. Many teachers allowed children to pursue their own programs and children were often given little direction, their own choice being paramount. This caused a degree of uncertainty resulting in a generation having less regard for adult views on behaviour generally and 'values' in particular.

- **Educational Theory**

There were two men who had a major influence on educational theory during the last fifty years Freud and Piaget, both formulating theories of how children move from the regulation of the adults who protect them in their early years, to a position of self-regulation. Necessarily their ideas must be compressed here but broadly speaking Freud believed in the existence of a super-ego, the mental controlling force which as it evolved replaced the externally imposed 'values' but yet retained much of them. Freud held this super-ego had two main features: the conscience which related to what was regarded as the adult's view of what is proper and improper the latter being punishable in one form or another, and the ego-ideal which incorporates what experience has shown will result in approval and reward.

Piaget, a Swiss psychologist, suggested there were, broadly speaking, three stages of development. The period in the first two years of life which he termed 'Sensory Motor Intelligence' the stage when a child is egocentric, organizing its view of the world basing learning on perception and manipulation but not using imagery yet.

From two until about ten the child moves through the early symbolizing stage using simple representation (including language). These processes of imagery, memory and language are the processes the child uses before it is capable of internalized thought - this Piaget defines as Concrete Operational because it is dependent on objects which are tangible and there is no generalization. At this stage the child needs new experiences to develop new concepts and cannot make links or leaps of thought without such experience.

When the child is able to reflect on previous thought processes and recognize relationships and hypothesize (usually about the age of eleven) it has reached the stage of true operational thought. This is when an individual is able to consider a problem from several angles internally assessing the alternative probabilities of 'success' or 'failure'.

The progression from one stage to another depends on stimulus and experience. Children raised without the necessary contacts and challenges rarely make substantial progress and development is often spasmodic and lacking in consistency so that the child may develop in one subject such as mathematics while not showing comparable development in language. Its take-up of different 'values' can be very variable.

Piaget held that a child can and will develop its own concept of what is 'fair' and 'just' and that there is an evolutionary process beginning with ideas of expiating behaviour moving on with growing social awareness to concepts of reciprocity. Meanwhile the initial recognition of the child's dependence on adults is gradually replaced by the increasing exposure and relationship with its peers. Moral and social development can only come with experience which leads to modification in previously held 'values' and for this to happen there must be an internalization of the meaning of that experience.

Young children are egocentric, selfish, seeing the world entirely from their own point of view and unable to allow other individuals' interests any priority over their own. And some adults never move beyond this stage. Truly internalized learning is the result of understanding and acceptance. It is vitally important for the adults on whom the child is dependent to provide a consistent and secure framework within which the child can feel secure. Children who lack this tend to be confused reacting in a self-preserving way by telling lies, excusing themselves, sacrificing others, not knowing what is expected of them and continuously seeking approval.

The greatest problem with providing a frame of reference for value judgments by teachers is the danger that it can conflict with the 'values' already caught at home from the parents. Most children however recognize very quickly that different rules apply in differing situations. If there is a substantial difference between the home and the school 'values' problems are likely to arise particularly over the imposition of penalties by the school staff for contraventions against the rules ordering acceptable conduct. Unless the parent(s) uphold the disciplinary authority of the school there is almost inevitable trouble and the child will soon learn to play one parent off against the other and either, or both, against the school. Simplistic and clear messages to the child are vital particularly in the early years and any appearance of conflict must end in confusion.

School life should give children an experience of values which they might otherwise not be exposed to and without such experience a child cannot make a balanced choice. However care must be taken to ensure that the child is sufficiently mentally developed to be ready for the challenge. This dichotomy is not soluble in simplistic terms.

- **Fair and Decent Behaviour**

The majority of children tend to absorb 'values' leading to behaviour which their culture or subculture, regard as 'fair', 'just' and 'decent' (although these particular labels may well not be applied and there can be wide variations in what these terms represent). This is an essential part of 'growing-up' and getting these early guidelines 'right' is surely more important than mastering the elements of formal education itself. It is these basic 'values' which will usually determine just how far the girl or the boy will accept their obligations to others and thus play a realistic part in maintaining the fabric of their own culture.

Individuals are likely to 'get on' better with others (and therefore be far more likely to establish and to maintain satisfying relationships) if they understand how 'values' are formed and modified. To do this each of us must be aware of, and understand (partially at least) the frequent distortions, dissimilations and deceptions commonly found in much human behaviour and learn to interact accordingly. For this we need 'values' which are reasonably firm but, up to a point, malleable.

This is particularly true of the interactions, very important ones usually, with members of the opposite sex since there is a major communication problem between the sexes stemming from the different 'values' instilled by family tradition and also by the educational system itself.

- **Developing an Individual Philosophy**

While each individual's genetic inheritance sets the limits within which our upbringing, and our education, enable new 'values' to be 'taken on board', it is nevertheless possible at an early stage of development to introduce new concepts which can then be 'caught' by the majority of developing minds.

Surely youngsters should, at a suitable stage, be given a realistic appreciation of our relationship with the Universe recognizing that no-one knows for certain its purpose (nor the reason for conscious life on this planet), so that all of our 'myths' regarding our origins, and any moral or spiritual 'cosmology' derived from them, must be regarded as provisional. This should lead to an acceptance of the fact that, since we cannot establish 'Absolute' principles leading to unquestionable 'right' values, the questions must be considered in a pragmatic way. The objective must be to find, as far as we are able, those 'values' likely to lead to behaviour enabling our group, and our culture, to thrive. In other words to introduce 'values' which represent (for that particular group and culture) a 'fair' and 'decent' view of each individual's 'rights' 'duties' and 'responsibilities'.

Such a generally acceptable set of 'values' is necessary for any society to function reasonably smoothly and effectively while still providing room for the changes necessary to meet the rapidly altering social and scientific conditions inevitably thrust on us by the results of the application of the Scientific Method.

If such changes in individuals' 'values' do not enable the culture, and the society, to adjust sufficiently smoothly then the group is likely to disintegrate taking its culture with it.

- **The Current Over Emphasis on Science**

Today, in the Western World, most Governments (and many educationalists particularly those with a vested interest in 'Science') are consciously, or unconsciously, biassed when setting priorities for the education of their pupils. As has already been stressed, the development of the Scientific method has provided humanity with such amazing power that the dangers arising from that very success are not fully appreciated. Our main problems nowadays arise far more from our lack of understanding of essential and critical 'values' enabling us to interact realistically with others. Properly appreciating this should help us to evaluate how the critical interaction of our 'interests' and 'values' works. I do not suggest this would automatically resolve all our major problems but it would, I consider, be more likely to help us to find mutually acceptable solutions to many, presently apparently, intractable problems.

Much of what has been written on the subject of Sociology and Education seems to have far too limited objectives so that in many schools an undue degree of importance is attached to a form of education which it is believed, perhaps rightly, will help to improve the child's standard of living enabling them to move away from the social class into which they were born. To be fair to such writers, this objective is very often the one taking top priority in many parents' minds.

Setting a main objective of worldly success, something which is undoubtedly backed by a very powerful human drive, inevitably stresses the material advantages likely to flow from a scientific and technical education and reasonable allowance must therefore be made for it. However any educationalist, setting out to persuade students to adopt what should prove to be rewarding objectives and priorities, should also, I suggest, give due weight to the need for a wider view to ensure that they, the students, get from their education, a proper grounding in the fundamental issues, a sound view of the realities of life.

This should be provided by a sensible presentation of the importance of the 'right' values so that students would not be left (as largely they are at the moment) to develop, largely unaided, their own view of the meaning of the society in which they live, their personal 'philosophy' often emerging by chance exposure to religious, ethical and philosophical ideas, without any significant guidance regarding basic facts. Such an approach calls for an appreciation by the educational authorities of the vital importance of some study of ethics and philosophy which should surely be part of the general educational process at an age when the importance of these matters can be better appreciated.

I am not suggesting any kind of attempt to impose a specific and universal set of 'values' (something which it seems likely genetic differences would soon subvert) but that all should be influenced, specifically, in favour of tolerance of others' interests and 'values' within the framework of a generally accepted set of laws and mores and that this should be regarded as an essential part of all education. Also that there are but few basic 'values' and they should be able to understand, sufficiently early in life, the need for compassion and for a 'fair' allowance for others' 'interests' and 'values'.

Religion, which used to provide the concepts from which we all initially created our own usually simplistic cosmology, has for many of us (in Western society but not so in much of the Islamic world) now largely ceased to play that crucial part in our lives so it is essential our educational system should be developed to fill the resulting moral and philosophical void.

While, therefore, it may well be that a scientific and technical education can lead to better material prospects, by themselves these advantages will not necessarily lead to a feeling of satisfaction and fulfilment, particularly in the longer term, so that if, as is likely in many cases, 'upwardly mobile' ambitions are not fully met, the almost inevitable sense of failure and frustration can well cast a shadow over middle and later life. If career success is made the principal objective this may well prove to be a barrier against creating a happy family life either by causing the couple to delay having children until too late or, alternatively, by making any children all too conscious they are of but little relative importance in their parents' eyes compared with the career goals the parents are concentrating on.

- **The Education of Disturbed Children**

Here it is worth referring to the experience of introducing new (and in nearly all cases) a 'fairer' set of 'values' to a special group of children. These are assessed by Local Education Authorities as so 'disturbed' and disruptive they cannot be tolerated in ordinary schools. As anyone who has had experience with the special schools for such disturbed children will recognize such children will often come from backgrounds where they have failed to get the love, care and attention necessary for a balanced development. There are obviously exceptions where genetic factors are the cause but in many cases it seems that disturbed parents lead almost inevitably to disturbed children. This does not mean that an economically 'poor' family necessarily provides a worse background since, fortunately, 'decent' values can be found at all social levels of society.

The majority of such disturbed children have therefore missed that vital sense of security, and reliable protection, which provide the comfort most children need particularly in their early, more vulnerable years. The sometimes outrageous behaviour of some 'disturbed' children is driven, more often than not, by the need to call attention to themselves and is, usually, an unconscious cry for help. These are the children who, for one reason or another, have failed to absorb (primarily from their parents or the other adults who provide their early nurture) 'values' enabling them, the children, to integrate readily into their group and culture. In particular they have been unable to absorb the 'values' which for most of us provide the basic 'rule-making' and 'rule-accepting' features of ordinary social life.

Provided there is no genetically caused problem experience shows that in the right kind of atmosphere, a considerable change can often be achieved in evoking trust enabling the children to absorb, to catch, new more socially suitable 'values' helping them to adapt themselves better to the essential rules of the society in which they must live.

- **Educational 'Values'**

Reverting now to the main theme of this Chapter - How does formal education (provided usually by adults other than the parents) influence the way the growing child absorbs new concepts (thus modifying those already learned from the adults who protected it in infancy) and so develop its own personal and individual 'values'? This is a vast and complex subject so that I can only highlight some of the more important aspects.

In our Western culture 'formal' education, at school, does not normally start until the child is at least four (often now five although nursery school may commence earlier) so that by the time most children start 'proper' school the twig has been well and truly 'bent' by the exposure he or she has had to the 'values' operating at home.

Here it is worth commenting on the loose generalization given in Herbert Spencer's quotation at the head of this Chapter. A more fruitful definition of the main purpose of education was given by a highly experienced headmaster who said :

'the objective of Education is to aid the development, both mental and physical, of the young, so that as adults, they can fulfil their potential to the full in the home, at work, at leisure and in the society in which they live and have their being'.

• The Formation of Character

It is, of course, impossible to measure how well any particular form of education achieves so ill-defined an end as 'the formation of character' or of preparing the young 'to fulfil their potential' but surely it must be accepted that character must be based upon 'proper values' if harm is not to be caused. Few people would question that both Hitler and Stalin had outstanding characters but those who experienced the 1930s, the 1940s and the following years would surely agree that much of the chaos and human misery of the middle of this century stemmed from their self-centredness and their 'distorted' 'values' associated, as they were, with outstanding 'characters'.

To be effective, any study of the way an educational system evokes 'character' would need to be able to distinguish between the effects of heredity, of early environment and of the educational system itself. To obtain fully significant results would take more than a single lifetime, far too long for such studies to be completed, analysed and then used effectively because of the rapid rate of change in the factors involved. For not only would the conditions have changed significantly but also the generally accepted objectives (and also the preferred forms of education) would almost certainly have altered substantially meanwhile.

The Chinese have a saying 'Call no man fortunate until he is dead' which brings out, forcefully, the fundamental fact that it is not until the end of life that the interplay between heredity, early family training and later education can satisfactorily be recognized. And that is far too late to be of any real use in helping to judge between one form of education and another even if the basic objectives could be agreed upon. All we can do therefore is 'to take a view' based often more on sentiment rather than on reason.

- **The Indian Civil Service before 1947**

In comparatively recent times, there has been one 'experiment', one classic example, where the long term effects of a particular form of education has been tested (without specific intent) and where the results can be both recognized and appreciated. This relates to the history of the Indian Civil Service which appears highly relevant to the present discussion of the effects of differing forms of education.

Until Partition, (i.e. for the better part of a century) the ICS was staffed by a small group of men, almost entirely the products of the British public school system, a form of education which aimed at instilling a set of 'values' based on the concept of 'service'. These 'values', stemming largely from Ancient Greek philosophy as taught by a series of outstanding Headmasters, stressed that individuals should accept the concept of their 'obligations' to society in return for their 'rights'. A point of view which today many seem to regard as so old-fashioned as to be quite unreal.

In broad terms the general 'values' of the culture the Service represented emphasized the importance of behaving 'decently', working for the overall good of the people they ruled rather than seeking their own self-interest, aiming at cooperation rather than competition. The result was a group of administrators (with, it should be remembered, exceptionally wide powers and influence) controlling a subcontinent containing a huge population split into a complexity of races, religions, and cultures involving a wide diversity of cultural 'values' (many diametrically opposed and very strongly held as the savage aftermath of Partition showed).

This ruling class proved to be amazingly free from the widespread corruption and intrigue something which had been a main feature of authority in the subcontinent up to the time the ICS was created. This was a feature typical of almost all other 'empires' (including the Russian Communist regime) where that kind of power was held by a small ruling class.

They were not saints, and were certainly not all perfect, nor did they ignore their own self-interest, but the 'values' which had been instilled into them by their families first, and then by their education, produced a period of stability and sanity which has been sadly lacking since, not only in the Indian subcontinent, but also in other areas (such as the Sudan and

Uganda) where, for a time, the influence of such public servants was effective in providing a secure framework within which ordinary people could live and thrive.

This form of Colonialism (today a dirty word for so many without first-hand experience of what actually happened) may well have proven irksome for the elite, better educated, nationalists who longed to get control of the power and influence to be obtained from forming the Government but, as the results have demonstrated, it did provide much greater security for the majority of the ordinary people.

It is indeed a rather wry comment on the effect of the spread of the English language (which itself carried with it certain 'values') that the better educated Indians were able to absorb the very principles of democracy which, finally, led to the end of the Raj.

Many of the members of the ICS held an extraordinary degree of power and the way in which they used that power responsibly makes, to my mind, nonsense of the oft-quoted dictum of Lord Acton that 'Power corrupts and Absolute power corrupts Absolutely.' The ICS 'experiment' demonstrated clearly that given certain 'values' power does not necessarily 'corrupt'.

I believe a time may well come when, with the growing threat of chaos, of the spread of Aids and of diseases such as pneumonic plague, together with the threats posed by the possession of atomic and other weapons of mass destruction by irresponsible dictators, the civilized world will no longer be able to accept the dangers inherent in unbridled 'self-determination' and a new class of 'administrators' schooled in the concepts of 'service' and responsibility will be required probably sponsored, and supported, by some international organization such as the United Nations. But unfortunately that time is by no means yet!

• The Difficulty of Mounting Controlled Experiments

As has already been said it is difficult if not impossible to mount effective tests of alternative forms of education. This has meant that investigators have largely been forced to concentrate on what happens while the children are at school and few, if any, studies have attempted the far more important task of determining how successful the educational 'system' is at producing rounded human beings (however that might be defined). At the moment there would seem to be no way of starting such meaningful controlled experiments.

As a result an attitude seems to have grown up similar to that of the scientists who take the line 'As far as I am concerned, if it cannot be measured it does not exist', an attitude which may have been productive in many of the 'hard' sciences but which loses its force when dealing with the human mind and with the 'values' which control behaviour.

As has already been mentioned in a small way, and to a very limited extent, the experience of some of the special schools designed to deal with the disruptive behaviour of certain children provides a partial exception. In the schools which only keep children to age eleven or twelve there is a 'character' test used to decide whether the special treatment the school has provided justifies the child going back into main stream education or whether he, or she, must still be kept in the special school system until their formal education is finished.

While the numbers are small (and it is impossible to distinguish clearly between the effects of the genetic factors, the home environment and the schooling process) it is clear that, in some cases at least, the school can and does 'correct (some of) the mistakes the parents have made'.

The school staff have a reasonably clear objective in terms of the 'values' they are seeking to impart and while each child is clearly a special case, a separate individual, they know they have the same (limited maybe) objective, namely so to change the child's 'values' so that he or she can adjust sufficiently well to mainstream education. In other words to enable him, or her, to come to terms with society's need for rule-making and rule-accepting, to learn to interact and to live with both teachers and other children some with their very different 'values'.

Many of the children are in desperate need of help and guidance. They have internalized so much emotional damage, have often been exposed to so much hostility and harsh treatment (or alternatively to so much neglect) that without help at this early stage their future almost inevitably lies in the realms of psychopathy, mental illness, drugs and criminality.

- **Normal Education and the Transmission of 'Values'**

In an Appendix there is an analysis of some of the factors in normal education which influence the transmission and/or absorption of 'values'. Many of the factors are intangible and lack any form of adequate measurement so that their importance becomes a matter of subjective judgement (dependent therefore on the 'values' of the investigator). In many of the experiments the juries are still out and no final judgement is yet in sight so that while no doubt the shape of the 'best' education is still in doubt (it almost certainly varies with the individual child) it is possible in some instances to come to an overall judgement. But certainly any consensus is still far away.

In Appendix A reference is made to the main technical and other factors influencing and determining the results of the School Experience.

Chapter 5

Ethics, Philosophies, Religions & Values

The main, pragmatic, purpose of philosophy, of ethics, of much of religion and of any morality derived from these disciplines must surely be to establish, or alternatively to modify, patterns of behaviour in particular ways. Ways which should, broadly speaking, help the members of that culture to interact more readily with one another minimizing the conflicts of interests inevitable in any society. This can only be achieved by instilling, or by later modifying, those individual and unique 'values' by which each of us assess what we consider our 'rightful' interests to be and then determine the importance we attach to the interests, often competing ones, of others.

In the case of religion this is but part of the story since theories about the nature of God, the purpose of the Universe and of our presence on Earth are an important, probably the more important part, of any studies aimed at producing a convincing and satisfying cosmology from which to derive the 'values' we believe to be 'right' and which should be communicated to our children.

- **The Nature and Purpose of God**

When in 1779 *David Hume* published his *'Discourses concerning Natural Religion'* he concluded, *'the cause or causes of order in the universe probably bear some remote analogy to human intelligence'* and the current consensus seems to show little or no change from that conclusion. Certainly there is no general agreement on the answer to this or to the two other fundamental questions of whether there is any purpose in the Universe intelligible to us and whether there is a reason for the presence of conscious life on this minor planet.

Some of the advanced mathematicians seem to believe that the form of order they are discerning bear some relationship, or interaction, with their elaborate concepts of the physical processes they are studying but whether this is derived from the nature of the Universe or whether it is due to the nature and constraints provided by their own mathematics is still unresolved. It seems this must remain an open question at least for the time being.

- **Moral Concepts**

Any attempt to examine philosophical ideas without involving the moral concepts for the development of which the philosophical theories were developed would be unreal. And to attempt to cover, not only all philosophies, but also the derived moral concepts would be impossible within the space of a single chapter but, given its central importance to the subject of this book something must be attempted. Inevitably there must be compromise which is unlikely to satisfy all and the objective must be to highlight what may reasonably considered to be the main points in the hope this will persuade, or provoke, others to further critical enquiry leading to a more convincing analysis.

- **What does 'Good' mean?**

Given we have no convincing knowledge of the reason for our existence we must start with the basic assumption that when we use moral terms such as 'good' they should have a meaning for each person. The question then is "What do we mean by 'good'?" and can we find a definition which will help us in our investigation aimed at producing a meaningful and acceptable moral framework. Sadly the answer seems to be 'No!'.

In his Principia Ethica, G E Moore wrote:- *'Philosophical questions are so difficult, the problems they raise are so complex, that no-one can fairly expect now, any more than in the past, to win more than a limited assent* (to any statement about them)'. He then analyses, very precisely, what he considers to be the prime subject with which Ethics is concerned namely the meaning of the word 'good'. He concluded it was impossible to define so that each individual had to rely upon their own conception stemming from their own 'values' which had been evolved by the interaction between the concepts they had 'caught' tempered by their personal experience.

His book contains much closely reasoned argument in which he draws attention to fallacies apparent in the philosophies put forward by many of his illustrious predecessors such as Locke, Kant and Mills. I am not competent to judge the effectiveness of his criticisms and only make this reference to his, to me, convincing work because it provides strong support for one of my main arguments namely that there are no, so far, discernible Absolutes and that all ethical 'values' are relative in their nature.

At the same time we must recognize that for any society to function effectively it must establish rules, laws, mores and customs which will aim at controlling the actions of those whose self-centredness is such they would disrupt that society if they were allowed to behave solely as they wish. No society can tolerate, unchecked, the serial murders, the abductors and rapists, the psychopaths whose main purpose in life is to seek self-satisfaction in cruelty to others.

It is worth quoting from one section of the book where Moore illustrates how loosely most of us use the word 'good' and of what little regard we have for its precise nature when we discuss philosophical questions. In this he emphasizes that judgments about 'good' will be of two kinds:-

They may assert that:

A. this unique property 'good' always attaches to the thing

B. the thing in question is a cause, or a necessary condition for the existence of other things to which this unique quality applies

He maintains these two types of ethical judgment are very different so that much of the misunderstanding is caused by too loose a use of the term. In ordinary language we recognize the difference between 'good as means' and 'good in itself', which are associated with 'value as means' and 'intrinsic value'. This means that when we judge something as 'good as means' we make a judgment with regard to causal relations - we judge that it will both have a particular kind of effect and that the effect will be 'good' in itself. However since we cannot be omniscient we cannot foresee what the ultimate effects of any action will be and, therefore, any judgment regarding the outcome of any action is necessarily provisional and limited.

We cannot say without reservation that *any* particular action is necessarily 'good' irrespective of its ultimate longer term effects. The colloquial saying 'Well it seemed a good idea at the time!' sums up well our very limited understanding of the full effects of any action no matter how 'good' we judged it to be at the time we decided on it.

In effect we are generalizing, believing that in certain likely (we consider) circumstances for a particular individual, or individuals, a certain (often ill-defined) action is likely to prove to be 'good' according to our (inevitably) biased assessment of their 'interests' and 'values'. Here as everywhere else in life we are dealing with probabilities and expectations which are almost always unquantifiable.

It is worthwhile drawing a distinction here between the nuances which are implied in the use of the four words 'good' and 'bad'/ 'right' and 'wrong' all of which are judgments made by individuals according to their own unique personal set of 'values' (which are largely influenced if not determined by their culture or subculture) whereas 'fair' and 'unfair', 'decent' and the opposite, contain, by their very nature, an appeal to a commonly held set of 'values' determined by the general culture of the society in which they live and have their being. These words imply a concept of tolerance of others' interests' and 'values' and are, therefore, likely to prove of greater assistance in providing a useful and effective guideline to constructive action. They are obviously not Absolutes but have a relative nature since what is held generally to be 'fair' and 'decent' action changes with time and circumstance.

While from time to time there have been claims that certain of the ethical concepts we have derived from the Ancient Greek culture originated in earlier Hindu civilizations (and it seems clear the Jewish Ten Commandments came from concepts held in esteem in Ancient Egypt as shown in their Book of the Dead) any realistic examination of the form of Western Ethics must surely start with the debates of the early Greek philosophers.

Before examining briefly their conclusions it seems sensible to establish a general perspective and framework. Thus moral philosophy has often been approached as if its history was secondary and only marginally important whereas the reality is that a study of the history reveals the use of a particular word to express a particular concept has changed, sometimes markedly, over the years. Some philosophers have written as if moral concepts were timeless and unchanging, necessarily having the same impact throughout history often implying they represent an intrinsic part of our mentality just waiting to be evoked.

In other words they imply there is a singular Language of Morals waiting to be discovered through new insights similar to the way that new mathematical techniques have been developed to help more sophisticated analyses of our understanding of the Universe.

Again some writers, while accepting that moral practices and moral judgments may and do vary from one society to another (and from person to person), have subtly assimilated differing moral concepts implying that although what in different cultures is held to be 'right' and 'good' admittedly varies from one culture to another, nevertheless roughly the same concepts of 'right' and 'good' are universal. In reality moral concepts change as society changes and such concepts are part and parcel of social life and are, indeed, a function of that society. There is no precise English equivalent for the Greek word usually translated as 'justice' which is not just a linguistic defect but rather that certain concepts in Ancient Greek speech do not correspond with parallel concepts in modern English. To fully understand and appreciate what the rules are which govern the use of such words one must be immersed in that particular society. And of course the concepts attached to those critical words change with time and circumstance.

There are certain basic linguistic concepts which do not change but these are so for one of two reasons - either they are part of an unchanging discipline such as mathematics or they are highly generalized concepts such as 'AND', 'OR' and 'IF'. But moral concepts do not fit into either category.

It is then a basic mistake to approach the history of ethics and 'morals' as if throughout time we have been 'homing in' on certain fundamental concepts, to approach the subject as if Plato, Hobbes and Bentham were all attempting to define the same thing when they wrote about 'justice'. For while it is true that what Plato said originally, and what Hobbes and Bentham wrote are linked (for there are continuities as well as differences), the meaning and the implications of the word to each was not the same. And inevitably philosophical discussion itself can and does lead to changes in the way moral concepts are applied.

Philosophy is therefore likely to be subversive of existing ideas regarding 'manners, morals and customs' for to introduce a new understanding of a concept and to change the world view are two sides of the same coin so that any study concerned with the role of philosophy and ethics in relation to conduct, and therefore to 'values', cannot be neutral and must, if accepted, have its effect.

• Attempting to Define 'Good'

Now asking moral questions is not the same as attempting to answer philosophical questions about morality since by concentrating on moral questions of a certain kind reveals the fact that to get a sensible answer will depend on how certain philosophical questions have been put and answered. This was the start of philosophical ethics in Ancient Greek society when it became clear the meaning of some of the key words was ambiguous. Social changes had made some behaviour, once acceptable, now questionable causing some to question the validity of ideas which had defined the moral framework of that earlier society. And these changes are reflected in Greek literature from the time of the Homeric writers until that of the Sophists.

The word 'agathos' which is the ancestor of our 'good' was originally associated specifically with the role of an Homeric nobleman - to be 'agathos', wrote W H Adkins *'one must be brave, skilful and successful in war and peace, one must possess the wealth, and in peace the leisure, which are at once the necessary conditions for the development of these skills and the natural reward for their successful employment'*.

Therefore in many Homeric contexts the word 'agathos' is not like our word 'good'. Homeric terms were not normally applied as moral comments are applied in our society. Excuses, praise and blame play quite different parts and it is not logical to enquire whether (in the Kantian sense) 'ought' implies 'can'. In Homer 'ought' in the Kantian sense is not to be found. The Homeric picture is not, of course, of a real society but an idealized one.

Between Homer and the writers five centuries later there was a great change in their myths about the order of the Universe and the Homeric myths reflect, in an idealized fashion, a society in which a closely defined form of functional organization is presupposed by the moral evaluative framework.

• Seeking Absolutes

In the later writers it is clear the effect of the development of the city states was accentuated by the increasing awareness of very different social orders such as the Persian. The impact of their invasion, of colonization, of the widening trade and travel revealed the diversity of the real world, that what was held 'good' in Egypt did not hold in Persia or in Athens so that to seek for Absolutes became relevant. The question now asked of any social practice or moral rule became 'Is it just part of the local custom or is it essentially a universal fact of nature?' Which is linked to the question, *'Is it open to me to live in a society which suits my 'interests' and 'values' or does the nature of humanity effectively set limits on what I can choose?'*

Which is precisely the question we ask today!

• Justice and Fairness

The concepts implied by the Greek word (loosely equivalent to our 'justice') involve a notion of 'fairness' in external relationships associated with a personal dignity in a way no single English word can convey and this original sense was largely undermined, or modified, by the growing appreciation that alternative social systems operated, apparently, equally effectively so that the question arose 'Does the intrinsic concept of 'justice' differ then from city state to city state? Does it hold only within a given community between citizens i.e. those of broadly the same social status and not to slaves? Or should it hold good in all conditions at all time?

So Thucidides writing of the revolution in Corfu said *'The meaning of words no longer had the same relation to things but was changed... as they thought fit. Recklessness was held to be loyal courage, prudent delay was cowardice, moderation was unmanly weakness, to know everything was to do nothing'*

- **The Sophists and Socrates**

The Sophists attempted to tackle the two problems simultaneously, that of determining just what various 'values' meant and, at the same time, determining how to live 'well' (in their city state). Therefore as each state has its own laws, conventions and usages, one had to study the prevailing order and adapt to it. Apart from 'success' there was no criterion of 'virtue' and no test of 'justice' other than that determined by the current practice of each individual city. This completely relativist approach was developed somewhat differently by Plato, who linked 'moral relativism' with general relativism in a theory of knowledge based on sense perception, reasoning there is no such thing as a 'hot' or 'cold' wind only one which to a particular individual seemed 'hot' or 'cold'. And the question then became not, 'What is justice?' but 'What is justice in Athens?' which of course clearly does not produce any Absolute.

- **Aristotle**

According to Aristotle, Socrates did not attempt to establish Absolutes but made his students question their ideas of 'values'. By this technique he established it was not possible to get any better definition from the Sophists and the Innovators than he could by examining common usage so that, in his view, establishing one's ignorance of Ultimates became the main moral objective. Plato, on the other hand, maintained that the basic knowledge of the meaning of the critical 'values' was already part of our intrinsic nature being brought into the open by experience acting as a philosophical midwife.

Socrates had raised the key ethical questions:-

How do we understand the concepts we use in appraisal and decision? What are the criteria for their correct application? Is established usage consistent and if not how can we escape that inconsistency?

Clearly if our moral concepts are concepts at all, if moral words are more than just words, there must be criteria for their use and they cannot be meaningful unless there are rules for their use, rules that can be taught and learned established as socially acceptable. However it does not necessarily follow that any investigation of how a concept is used in different social milieu will necessarily provide one clear and consistent answer.

In Socrates time, the problematic moral character of Greek life arose largely from the fact that the usage of moral terms had ceased to be clear and consistent, which created the need for an attempt to establish some unambiguous and practical definitions of moral concepts. He considered to do this effectively, a different sort of enquiry was necessary. Plato, accepting that moral concepts are intelligible only against the background of a particular social order, then tried to define those concepts attempting, at the same time, to provide a justification for his views in terms of what he visualized to be the order of the Universe. Apparently the first attempt known to us to find what Plato called Universals and which we might equate with Absolutes.

Socrates did state one necessary condition for the answer to the question *'What does 'good' consist of?'* His view was that *'for something to be 'good' (and therefore a possible objective of desire)* it must be *specifiable in terms of some set of rules governing behaviour. An injunction to break all rules cannot make sense, for a man whose behaviour was not rule-governed in some way would cease to participate as an intelligible member of human society.'*

This indicates that 'badness' consists of a breach with a form of life in which certain 'goods' can be achieved for to share concepts is to share a form of life in some degree and Socrates says specifically that what a 'bad' man lacks is an ability to share common life (which in my terms could be regarded as an inability for his/her 'values' and 'interests' to interact satisfactorily with others) so that an essential step must be to create the kind of common life necessary for the 'good' to be realized. In Plato's views what he designated as the FORMS (which appear to approximate to Ultimates or Absolutes) were to be established, by reasoning, by a small group of philosophers, something which in the light of experience, appears highly unlikely and probably very unsatisfactory although, I suppose, that in a democracy of our kind we live under the illusion that is what Parliament aims to do.

This fundamental point of view, the necessity for 'rules', was later explored by Wittgenstein who argued there must be such rules recognized as socially desirable practices whereas St. Augustine held the view that such ideas and concepts came from *'an interior illumination from God'* a point of view which is, today, unacceptable by many.

- **Free Will**

With regard to the question which troubles much modern discussion - Are all actions determined by causes independent of the agent's choice? Aristotle argued there must be a distinction between agents acting under exterior compulsion, or ignorance, and those not so acting. In his view this established deliberation and choice as key factors for deliberation (which I suggest infers interaction of 'values' and 'interests') concerning 'means' and not necessarily 'ends'. Surely deliberation of this sort can only relate to things which can be changed and therefore indicates it must be about 'means'.

He also argued that not all voluntary actions are 'chosen' for every action should be assessed in the light of what a 'prudent' man would decide where 'prudent' has a very specialized meaning, being the qualities a man shows when he *'knows how to apply general principles in a particular situation' - not just the ability to formulate principles and to deduce from them what should be done but rather the ability to act so that 'right' principles take a concrete form.'* Something which today would, I consider largely be covered by our use of the words 'decent', 'fair' and 'seemly' used to describe behaviour.

It is interesting to note he believed that an explicit and articulate grasp of 'principles' would help to determine the 'right' sort of conduct whereas some later writers such as Tolstoy and

D H Lawrence considered that too explicit a statement of principles could easily be 'morally crippling' holding that intuitive behaviour was, from the point of view of the individuals concerned, much to be preferred. This different approach is perhaps due to the fact that Aristotle was more concerned with the 'good' of society whereas the other writers were more concerned with the 'good' of the individuals involved in the decisions and therefore rated the emotional factors higher in importance than the more mental and rational ones.

Here it may be helpful to refer back to an earlier chapter in which a distinction was drawn between 'values' which had a biological basis and others which referred and related more to the social and communal origin - the distinction is brought out well by the old saying 'Everything is fair in love and war!'

- **Moral Failure**

Human desires are rarely straightforward drives to unambiguous goals in the way that biologically based needs tend to be. Desires are expressed in terms of goals and we use our 'values' to assess our interests and, after allowing more or less for the 'interests' and 'values' of the others we consider important to us, then to reach after those goals. If individuals always did what they thought was 'best' for all there would be little to determine in terms of moral success or failure but obviously this is not so in real life. Fallibility is an essential part of human nature partly because the differences between individuals' 'values' prevent us from understanding and appreciating the goals of others and partly because of our self-interest.

- **Ethics and 'Values' - Finale**

This review of the early history of the Greek development of ethics and philosophy was designed to establish clearly that, from the beginning of Western thought on the subject, the relative nature of the concepts involved was recognized and largely accepted by the rationalists. It is not practicable to deal in similar detail with the following history but it seems fair to say that, apart from those claiming particular insight from God, no-one has been able to establish a convincing set of Absolutes although it is generally now accepted that there are certain biological factors which humanity must recognize and embrace if their race and their culture is to prosper and survive.

It is true that in 'the Century of Enlightenment', many Western thinkers believed it was possible through reasoning to determine final definitions of 'right' and 'wrong' their motto being 'dare to know' rejecting the authority of the Church, but experience led to growing doubt and uncertainty leaving us in a state of something approaching moral confusion since we now lack the firm guidance from both revelation and reason.

The ideas set out in this book, which I have culled from many sources, stress therefore the relativity of the 'value' factors influencing if not determining our actions, they underline our present dilemma and offer an approach to 'humanistic' 'values' aimed at adjustments to our ways of thinking and our forms of education, accepting the importance of people rather than objects and of 'value' rather than price.

What is set out does not seek to provide a panacea for our ills but should, properly handled, offer an approach which should help to reduce some of the constantly increasing tensions both inside our own culture and outside in its conflicts with others.

To end this Chapter very much where it started I quote G E Moore's contention that the basic purpose of ethics is to define, and to establish, what is meant by 'good' and since this concept is indefinable we are forced to the conclusion that in practical terms, in real life, we are concerned with our own peculiar and unique 'values' which must be and always will remain relative. No-one has the ability to decide what is 'right' and 'wrong' using their own 'values' alone, all they can say is that they judge some possible action is, in their opinion, likely to be 'good' or 'bad' for them. This does not of course remove the need for each society, or culture, to establish communal concepts of what is 'fair' and 'decent' but these too will vary from time to time and from place to place.

But more of this in the Finale.

Chapter 6

Behaviourism & Body Language

Behaviourism can be regarded as an attempt to establish a 'science' of human behaviour. It considers whether such a 'science' is practicable, to what extent it can cover all aspects of human behaviour, what methods of study should be used, whether an effective technology can be established and if so what part can it play in human affairs. Behaviourism sets out to provide a detailed report on how our 'values' interact to result in behaviour. It is a complex subject and only a short outline is practicable here.

Much of the behaviourist reasoning is difficult to follow but an examination of the arguments currently put forward in its favour provide a useful supplement to the study of 'values'. It must be remembered that Behaviourism concentrates on actual behaviour largely leaving the origins of that behaviour to other disciplines.

- **Mental Events Unobservable**

There is one major problem since no two observers can agree on exactly what happens in the world of the mind. Mental events are 'unobservable' so that for those scientists who argue that 'what can't be measured is not fit for study and analysis' such studies are unreal. An early attempt to provide some kind of measurement for comparative purposes led to a branch of behaviourism described as 'Methodological Behaviourism' which, while accepting the existence of mental events, ruled them out of consideration holding there were two worlds one of the mind and the other of matter and that the two did not interact. There is however a wealth of evidence to the contrary much of it stemming from our own personal experience.

- **Radical Behaviourism**

A later version, 'Radical Behaviourism' suggested that, in this area, 'truth' does not necessarily depend upon universal agreement. It therefore accepted the reality and importance of mental processes. It just questioned the nature of the 'object' observed and the 'reliability' of the observation stressing that what is felt, or introspectively observed, is not necessarily the 'cause' of behaviour. Any living organism behaves as it does because of its structure most of which not being subject to introspection. What is important is an individual's genetic and environmental history and what is introspectively observed is only a product.

This means that while environment is a major determining factor during the evolution of the species it exerts an effect of a different kind during the lifetime of the individual. Gene inheritance is of vital importance in determining an individual's 'qualities' and the combination of the two: the effect of environment on the species over time and the effect of current environment on the individual largely determines behaviour.

'Environment' includes, of course, other humans both living and (to a diminishing extent with time) dead. We are all, constantly interacting with the mental environment created by the 'values' of others, consciously or unconsciously, through body language, speech, books, radio, television and now, computers.

• Environmental Effects

Humanity is inevitably deeply concerned with mental life. With the comparatively recent appreciation of the importance of the evolutionary concept it is time to consider what effect 'environment', in its widest sense, has on 'values' and 'interests' and therefore on behaviour. We are all 'culture bound' and therefore cannot approach the subject of behaviour without prejudices which are part of the words we use to establish a realistic picture of what is happening. In this area of what happens in the mind, we have no clear definitions which enable us to communicate precisely. It is therefore useful to analyse the way we use words dealing with the interaction of thought and action so loosely.

While this problem is involved in all statements it does not invalidate all attempts to pursue the investigation. It must however be kept firmly in mind since most of the time we are dealing with 'ideas' not with 'facts'.

• Analysis and Speculation

Much of what is written is, therefore, necessarily speculative and speculation which cannot be put to the test of experimental verification does not normally form part of science. If this approach was regarded as an essential feature for investigation generally much of astronomy and of atomic physics would be considered unscientific.

Since the words we use reflect the way we think and most of us believe most of our actions are controlled by our minds it is necessary for the behaviourist to 'look through' our immediate thoughts to see what has given rise to them.

• Physiological Factors

First consider some physiological facts regarding our bodily responses - apart from the systems which preserve us biologically there is, for humans another arising from 'verbal' interactions. Questions require answers which provide useful information helping to anticipate other people's likely attitudes and actions.

While we assume that each of us can accurately describe our bodily state this is a misapprehension for, normally, it is impossible to experience what is currently happening to someone else.

Again we sometimes use confusing wording to tell about behaviour since for 'Current Behaviour' we might answer the question; What are you doing? by giving an answer which gives the other person information which is important to them or to the person giving the reply.

Then there is 'Probable Behaviour' when information is given indicating a probability and further there is 'Perceptual Behaviour' where the information relates to something observed by both and is given to clarify the reality.

All this emphasizes the vague nature of any verbal communication we make so that any attempt to find the causes of a particular form of behaviour suffers from these difficulties in observing and recording any results obtained. There are material differences between behaving, reporting behaviour and analysing the causes of behaviour even when the individual is well balanced and is striving to help.

- **Self-Knowledge**

The act of 'knowing' must imply an audience for it is only when the private world becomes of importance, that self-knowledge becomes important, since we are then better able to control our interaction with others as we perceive them to relate to us.

The behaviourist recognizes the importance of introspection in considering past actions and the reasons for it. Current action (or inaction) and present conditions and also the conditions likely to affect future actions.

There is a useful comment that nothing is different until it makes a difference and we lack the concepts to be precise with regard to what happens in the mind. Since Plato's time mentalism has dominated our thinking so that we assume, blindly it seems, the 'mind' differs from the brain holding that it operates non-physically.

- **Consciousness**

This concept is so much part of our conditioned thinking that to question what it means seems unreal but any attempt to define exactly what it is seems little better today than when Plato first suggested the concept. Present day psychology has perhaps opened up some areas but any proper understanding of what 'consciousness' is seems as far away as ever. The best the 'behaviourist can do is to put forward some suggestions on the way people respond to their mental activities. For instance the suggestion of instincts as 'driving forces' has been shown to be a misleading approach the reality being that certain behaviour could better be described as having sustaining or destructive consequences.

The behaviourist reply to the question, why did the mind (or for that matter 'values') develop, would be to suggest it is a meaningless question since it could only be answered realistically if we knew 'Why' we are here.

• Experience and Reality

It is clear from many experiments that what we 'perceive' at different times in different conditions is not simply a matter of a physical reaction but that our mind operates on the physical information it receives to 'perceive' one pattern or another. In a somewhat similar fashion looking at and considering the same action can and will be interpreted very differently by individuals with different sets of 'values' and, certainly at the moment, there seems to be no way to establish an independent 'truth' especially with regard to motives.

• Probabilities & Truth

People assess probabilities, often subconsciously, and when this is linked with the advantage or disadvantage we attach to the particular action this becomes an 'expectation' which then becomes an important factor leading to action or inaction.

When someone makes a statement the hearer has to make an assessment (usually instantaneously) on whether the speaker 'knows' the truth, whether he/she wants the hearer to know the 'truth' and how reliable the speaker is in assessing the relevant facts. Experience is the only way to obtain some idea of probabilities and expectations of this kind, and even with experience the 'truth' is hard to establish.

At the same time 'reliability' in reporting and acting is an important factor in the social cement which binds any community together.

- **The Structure of the Mind**

Lacking adequate information regarding an individual's early environment (particularly their interaction with the adults who provided the early nurture essential for their survival) it seems inevitable that important aspects of the mind's operation are considered to be of genetic origin. There is an argument that our greatest achievements are so recent in historical time that a genetic origin is inconceivable, but that surely is but part of the story. The example of a child violinist playing a complicated piece of music superbly at the age of eight must surely provide some evidence that the genetic factors are very important.

Many behaviourists question the existence of the 'mind' as such arguing that human 'thought' is just another aspect of human behaviour and certainly if this simplistic line is taken it avoids many of the philosophical problems which have beset many of the leading thinkers since Plato first started the debate.

- **Reasoning**

Humanity seems to have developed a form of brain which more readily recognizes patterns and similarities rather than chaos although of recent years this too has become a subject for investigation. We are conditioned to analyse and, as far as we can, extract 'rules' helping us to forecast the future with greater accuracy. The elaboration of the Scientific Method is the classical example of this. Problems can be solved by finding the conditions that lead to a general rule which holds good for all but the extreme ends of the likely distribution and, using such rules, the expectation of getting a 'satisfactory' answer is then greatly improved. This does not mean the rule will always prove to hold good only that using it will provide the 'best' expectation.

• Personality & 'Values'

In behaviourist terms an individual's 'values' could be described as a repertoire of behaviours responding to various contingencies. The early 'values' acquired in infancy represent one facet or level being one 'self', while the overlying 'values' acquired later represent another, the two selves coexisting until changes in circumstances cause a confrontation when personality problems may well develop. Our 'values' stem from the culture in which we live and if the society which inculcated those cultural 'values' loses its coherence then the individual's 'values' can disintegrate and the behaviour of some individuals becomes unpredictable.

Differing and conflicting stresses evoke different lines of behaviour so that someone who in their normal milieu is considerate can, if frightened, behave callously. What a person 'is really like' (meaning their inherited character) is a meaningless enquiry.

The behaviourist analysis is that as a species we are concerned with survival and reproduction and certain of our 'values' have evolved for thus purpose while as individuals we have acquired individual and personal 'values' in accordance with our own experience.

• Summing Up

The old saying 'Actions speak louder than words' provides a useful start to a summary of the behaviourist position. For understanding what humanity needs to achieve that zest for life which makes living fulfilling and worthwhile. Man is unique in being a 'moral' animal i.e. in having 'values'. We have developed a wide variety of such 'values' which guide our actions and interactions and we switch from one repertoire of 'values' to another (mostly without conscious thought) dependent upon how we assess our relationships by those 'values'. When someone is unsure what set of 'values' should be used they can become confused acting impulsively and often aggressively.

Finally the central issue is that of autonomy - to what extent are we in control of our future? Man's most conspicuous achievement is his mastery over his environment which has resulted in the population explosion which, unless it is sensibly controlled, must lead to disaster. Thus our very success in mastering our environment will, it seems inevitably, provide breeding ground for problems both in the Third World and in the more developed countries which only a major change in our 'values' will enable us to avoid. Behaviourism should help by providing an approach to a more scientific understanding of the roots of behaviour. It does not 'reduce' thought processes into behaviour but seeks to relate behaviour to the earlier thought processes.

Similarly it does not 'reduce' morality into reactions to the social environment but insists that those features are a factor in moral behaviour. It could be regarded as reductionist for it aims at analysing social processes in terms of the behaviour of individuals but this can well be regarded as giving individuals more rather than less importance.

• Body Language as Part of Behaviourism

Clearly our body language (including the tone of voice) is part, often a very significant part, of our behaviour since it is an important factor in amplifying, or modifying, the spoken word thus conveying to others important information about our values and how we view the relationship between what we regard as our own interests and our likely action resulting from our perception of their's.

Again this is a subject which requires more detailed treatment than is practicable here and some of the more important factors are considered in Appendix B.

FINALE

We Have too many Men of Science, too few Men of God. We have Grasped the mystery of the Atom and Rejected the Sermon on the Mount....Ours is a World of Nuclear Giants and Ethical Pygmies. We know more about War than about Peace, more about Killing than about Living...Humanity is trapped in this World by Moral Adolescence.

General Omar Bradley 1948.

Judging by what has happened in Chechnya, Bosnia, the Sudan, Ruanda and many other parts of the world, 'Man's inhumanity to Man' persists virtually unchanged so that the last forty-five years have not materially improved the conditions described by General Bradley's graphically worded comments which he made shortly after the end of World War II. We urgently need, therefore, some basic changes, indeed a revolution, in the way we perceive the world, and our place in it, in order to find a generally acceptable way to start to transform that 'moral adolescence' into something more approaching 'moral maturity'. Given today's wide disparity of cultures and, therefore, of 'values', this is an immense and daunting task and there is no easy solution.

Keeping the General's all too accurate and painful comment in mind, the time has come to review the material contained in the earlier chapters to assess the 'facts' which have emerged, and to indicate some conclusions which can reasonably be drawn from them. It is important to emphasize that word 'reasonably' because, for most of us, in such matters emotion is at least as important as reason especially so in fundamental areas such as the myths and 'values' derived from religion and nationality where, for most people, emotion is, by far, the more powerful influence. Reason conflicting with myths can provide an explosive mix as Darwin found when he was finally persuaded to publish his 'Origin of Species'.

Clearly there are two forms of 'values', those which operate (in a general way) in a given society or culture as a whole and others which relate to individuals these being primarily determined, or controlled, by their genetic inheritance. These two are so intermingled, so interdependent, that it is often difficult to disentangle them. However it is possible to distinguish certain types of 'value' which have more importance in terms of society as a whole and others which, self-evidently, have a greater impact at the level of the individual.

Thus acquired 'values' are likely to be of greater importance in terms of the general needs of society while biologically based 'values' will be so for the individual, although any society which ignores the latter is likely to find it far more difficult to gain acceptance for its laws and mores. Our acquired 'values' are often needed to control the urges which our biological inheritance sometimes drives us to express, on occasion with devastating effect. There are, of course, some biologically based 'values' such as those stressing the importance of the family unit in providing suitable child care which are, in the longer run, as vital to the health of the community as they are to the family itself.

Given General Bradley's stress on Christ's teaching as expressed in the Sermon on the Mount it seems worthwhile to examine what might be regarded as a reasonably current Christian point of view. Using the list of 'the values to live by' according to one active preacher of the Christian Gospel we find:-

1. Love God with all your heart, mind and soul.

2 & 3. Love your neighbour as yourself; Treat all others as you wish to be treated by them.

4 & 5. Follow Jesus' example and forgive as you wish to be forgiven.

6. Be faithful in all your dealings.

7, 8 & 9. Pursue peace with all; Seek mildness, kindness and self-control; Return evil for evil to no man; Do not let the sun go down on your wrath.

10 & 11. Do not steal; Do not murder; Do not bear false witness.

12. Do not covet your neighbour's possessions.

When these are considered carefully, it will be seen that the fundamental 'values' for interacting with others must lie in 2 & 3, to 'Love thy neighbour as thyself' for all the other 'commandments' are variations, or amplifications, of this. But while this undoubtedly provides an admirable general precept it does not provide an effective guide for dealing with what is commonly viewed as 'evil' behaviour either in personal relationships or in the body politic.

• THE PROBLEM OF EVIL

If we commence, as I consider we should, by accepting Shakespeare's 'Nothing is either good or bad but thinking makes it so' as providing a useful starting point we must be forced to conclude that it must be both false and misleading to hold there is something 'out there' which is 'evil'. 'Evil' is a 'value' judgment which can only be properly applied to human behaviour and therefore to human 'values'. To treat it as something having an existence of its own quite apart from humanity must confuse the real issues. Surely the reality is that some people, for one reason or another, behave towards others in such an antisocial way that most of the members of their community label them as 'evil'. I suggest that these are mostly the ones (those falling within the 'lunatic fringe' of the 'values' distribution) whose genetic make-up is such that they are unable to absorb, to 'catch', the 'values' which the remainder of their group regard as 'decent' this failure resulting in behaviour which the group has good reason to label 'evil'. This point of view is supported, in part at least, by the current argument that there may well be a regressive gene affecting and influencing antisocial behaviour.

This genetically 'impoverished' group was, for me, admirably described in 'A Tan & Sandy Silence' by the American crime writer John D MacDonald who wrote:-

'He fits the pattern... (and) could be called the activated sociopath sadist... Excellent in areas requiring ritual... Quite cold inside... Unable to concede the humanity of people around them because, having no basis of comparison, they think all of us have their same dry and barren soul... He isn't aware of evil... You have to think of him as a bored child who suddenly

discovers it is wonderful fun to go to the pet store and buy a mouse and bring it home and do things to it until it is dead. Life is no longer boring. It is full of rich and wonderful excitement. The mouse shares the experience, so he is fond of the mouse for as long as it lasts. He loves the mouse to the extent he can feel love... He is not a madman in any traditional sense. He cannot feel guilt or shame. If caught he would feel (only) fury and indignation at his game being ended too soon.'

Such people cannot be treated with the tolerance which is both reasonable and proper for others whose 'values' fit into the more common patterns which can be typified as 'decent' according to the society/culture in which they live. It is to control the effects of this type of deviant behaviour that each society establishes limits, rules and forms, some kind of legal system, to protect its members from the actions of the 'lunatic' fringe. Thus 'tolerance' itself must have its limits if society is to function reasonably effectively. It is not an Absolute in itself.

• INFANT DEPENDENCY

While the simplistic view of 'nature red in tooth and claw' has, today, given way to a recognition that, in the case of a mammal such as Homo Sapiens with such a long dependency before the newly born infant can survive on its own, the cooperation of others, and particularly of other adults, is vital if both the infant, and therefore the group, is to continue to exist - the equally important instinct for self-survival is still the key to many actions and interactions. So while the commandment 'To love others as oneself' conforms, in part, to an essential ingredient in the human psyche it is almost always at odds with an equally powerful biological directive to ensure the safety and wellbeing of the individual concerned.

Surely it was Christ's message that we should be tolerant of other's 'values' to an extent which was not visualized by most of the religious teachers of his day which helped to persuade the disciples, and the crowds, to accept him as divinely inspired.

It is one we must respect, and give priority to, especially in those areas such as the protection of children upon which the survival of the genus and our particular culture must depend.

Turning now to a survey of what has already been written in the earlier chapters:-

• EARLY DEVELOPMENT

At birth each baby is primarily an alimentary tube concerned solely and utterly with survival. Initially the overwhelming priorities are the physical ones to feed, to excrete and to seek comfort. All impressions of the world must be chaotic so that while there are certain biological needs there is nothing which can in any way be regarded as 'values'. Slowly each baby acquires a 'world view', a primitive cosmology, which involves interaction with adults and their differing 'values'. The infant has to develop an initially simplistic mental view of its immediate surroundings and then, slowly, of the physical world which envelopes it especially of the other humans with whom it is in direct contact, primarily its parents or other such adults who provide the succour and protection necessary for the infant to survive.

As has already been said it learns, quickly in some cases, more slowly in others, that some of its behaviour is (from the point of view of those adults and primarily from its mother, or acting mother) 'good' and others 'bad' so that initially what those adults indicate is 'good' becomes 'right' and what they say is 'bad' becomes 'wrong'. As time goes by these crude 'values' (which initially largely relate to physiological processes) are modified and tempered by the sometimes very different 'values' of their peers and of the other adults (family, friends, teachers) whose views impinge on the nurture of the growing child. All this taking place within the culture of its particular environment. Today these influences come from a wide variety of sources such as printed material, radio, television and, increasingly, computer output. This is in addition to the far more immediate and direct interaction with the humans, adults and others, with whom it is normally in continuous contact.

- **INTERACTION OF 'VALUES'**

Each individual inherits a unique genetic pattern which provides differing degrees of sensitivity to others enabling that individual to play, more or less successfully, the multi-dimensional chess game of human relationships, playing largely unconsciously and often without the need for analysis or specific consideration. Rather like the different power and influence of different chess pieces other individuals provide different interactions while, to complicate matters still further, in real life these other individuals can and do change their importance, sometimes dramatically and almost instantaneously. Social relationships are both physical and mental, they are TRANS-actions calling for a level of intelligence and communication unparalleled in any other living form. This is the human game we start to play as babies and which goes on as long as we live and retain our faculties. Those who are good at it we have learned to call 'wise'.

• THE SCIENTIFIC REVOLUTION

With humanity's ever increasing power over its environment, a power which we are starting to develop into a control of our own genetic inheritance, the previous limits on space and time have largely disappeared. The insulation which space used to provide so that in different parts of the world different cultures (embodying different sets of 'values') could develop, sometimes to disappear without any effect on cultures in other parts of the globe, no longer exists. It is still true that what happens to an aborigine in Australia is unlikely to be of immediate importance to someone living in the Midwest in the USA, but if an oil-rich dictator gets control of intercontinental ballistic missiles with atomic warheads it could well make a vital difference to the survival of Western culture. The spread of Aids to Third World countries with their teeming growing populations could well have a greater effect than all the Malthusian polemics we have heard so far.

As yet we have not come to terms with the results of our far greater control over our physical environment especially our ability to communicate almost instantaneously and our 'values' have not yet been tailored to the implications of the inevitable changes in our mental environment. 'To love one's neighbour' has an entirely different meaning today to that it held when Christ walked this earth. In today's global village who is not 'our neighbour'?

• Historic Perspectives

To place this in proper perspective it is necessary to reflect that, while Homo sapiens (and therefore some form of body and other language) goes back something like 100,000 years (say four to five thousand generations), anything which can be recognized as 'civilization' probably started less than 10,000 years (i.e. 400 generations) ago, Western civilization spanning only say three to four thousand years (at the most two hundred generations).

This means our modern culture (based mainly on the Scientific Revolution) relates only to say 250 years (i.e. ten generations at the most) to see that the frightening need to adapt our 'values' to today's ever more rapidly increasing power over both our environment, and ourselves, has led to problems for which the great majority of humans are quite unprepared. And we still give the study of science and the scientific method top priority in most of our schools and many of our universities at the expense of the 'humanities'!

- **RELIGIONS, PHILOSOPHIES, COSMOLOGIES & MYTHS**

In a (to us) recognizable form, written language seems to have started somewhere about six thousand years ago. While therefore there could have been some consideration, and analysis, of 'values' before the written forms were developed the effect was likely to be transient although the myths regarding the origin of the universe, and of life on this planet, would seem to go back as far as we can trace. Certainly in nearly all the primitive races there are such myths which have been handed down in the spoken word (or in dance form) from the earliest days. Without some form of communication, of language, such myths (the earliest forms of cosmologies) could scarcely have existed and without some form of cosmology there could have been little, if any, scope for expressing the concept of 'values' as we understand them although, in any group of mammals, there are likely to have been rules enabling the group to adhere and to survive.

All studies of the wide variety of mythologies of which we are aware confirm the unity of humanity not only in biological terms but also in what might be termed its spiritual inheritance. It would seem that, some at least of the earliest members of Homo sapiens, were conscious of the possibility of something beyond their immediately present world; the essence of nature, the spiritual world of their ancestors, the power of the gods, often seeking to attribute human 'values' to non-human entities. The disposition to some form of religious belief is one of the most powerful and complex forces in the human mind and may well be an ineradicable part of human nature. It has been one of the universals of social behaviour in every society of which we have record, from the hunter-gatherer wandering bands to the latest New Age travellers. It is our response to our common need to believe we are not just 'A Cosmic Jest'.

Indeed standards of ethics (and the implied morality) expressed in the form of human 'values' seem to be an almost inevitable product of human evolution since altruism, to a greater or lesser degree, is part of the behavioural pattern of social animals and can therefore be expected to be developed much further in the intelligent and intensely social beings such as our human ancestors.

We are cultural creatures to an extent, unmatched by any other species and the generation to generation transmission of ideas and of 'values' means that we are all involved in the cumulative development and expression of our particular species so that we are the beneficiaries of our ancestors, both immediate and distant, in a way not experienced by any other species. That is probably the most important single behavioural trait in human history - the transmission of culture in general (and of 'values' for individuals in particular) from generation to generation provided the folklore encapsulating the accumulated 'wisdom' essential for survival in the earliest days and providing also an acceptable cosmology, helping successive generations to come to terms with the world around them without having to hammer this out afresh in each generation. It so happened that, nearly always, the transmitted 'myth' explained and justified the existing form of society. Often such 'myths' provided some concept of a life after death usually designed to accentuate those 'values' having a beneficial social influence.

What people needed, and therefore sought, was an acceptable explanation of 'Why?' and 'How?' which usually came in the form of a myth - not one normally based upon demonstrable fact but as an Authorized story which the dictionary definition of 'myth' (a sacred narrative explaining how the world and humans came to have their present form) makes quite clear.

Now when scientists are asked if they can suggest any answer to the question 'Why?' they are likely to answer (as Richard Dawkins does in 'River out of Eden') that this is a nonsensical question. Life in general and our conscious life in particular are here and they do not have to have a 'Purpose'.

That is all very well if one is taking a detached scientific view of the 'occurrence' of life but it seems to be part of our mental make-up, part of our psyche, that we need to have, or to construct, some kind of purpose for our existence, some explanation of just why we are here.

Since we cannot it seems provide a convincing and rational answer to that fundamental question of 'Why?', for the time being at any rate, we must accept that here we are and here we stay while we are alive so we must make the best of it and get on with our lives, enjoying them to the full as far as we can, without harming others as far as that lies in our power.

Perhaps a humdrum answer to the quintessential philosophical question but, it seems, the best that offers at the moment !

• LANGUAGE

Probably the major event in the evolution of culture was the development of a fully articulated spoken language. That 'fully articulated' is important because Neanderthal Man, our probable predecessors, were apparently not physically equipped (in terms of their vocal structure) to produce the wide range of sound enabling the use of the more sophisticated language homo sapiens began to develop. Our sense of morality, fairness/equity, transcendental vision and 'values' all seem to stem from this very special gift. However recent work on the higher primates together with the studies of the fossil and archeological record of human pre-history, indicate we are the end-product of an evolutionary unbroken lineage which links us to the rest of the natural world.

In other primates the ultimate driving force would seem to be the need for reproductive success, the female striving to raise to maturity as many offspring as they can while the males strive to father as many as they can. For both males and females their objectives are likely to be eased if they can rely upon the support of at least some other adults (relatives or friends) so that a good deal of primate life is spent in nurturing long term or short term alliances and of assessing the strength of the alliances of rivals, a complex process requiring quite sophisticated cognitive abilities.

Language, and with it human consciousness, culture and 'values' emerged gradually through history. Each of the homo species antecedent to Homo sapiens had a measure of humankind about it and each had elements of humanness in the way their minds worked which helps to place our undoubted 'specialness' in a proper perspective.

• CONSCIOUSNESS & DEATH

It would seem that we are unique among living species in our appreciation of 'death', an appreciation stemming from our sense of consciousness something we have, so far, not been able to discern in other species. All this stems from the complex web of relationships between our physical abilities, our brains/minds/ intelligence and our linguistic abilities. Our ability to interact and to respond must have started in the earliest days of our existence and these basic lessons in survival (often in an hostile environment) taught the need for cooperation leading, in time, to rules for conduct, of morals and of 'values' necessary for the later more complex forms of society to be developed and maintained.

• THE URGE TO KNOW

With the birth of consciousness came the urge to know and, to a material extent, we have created the world we live in for art and scientific thought; culture and 'values' all stem from human consciousness. It is consciousness which makes each of us feel unique but this can lead to an arrogance, to an anthropocentric view of the universe. In fact this attribute is a fragile entity, a cognitive illusion created by some neural trick in our brain. While we may well find it difficult to accept, it is at least possible, if not likely, that the human mind has definite limits to what we are able to comprehend and our own consciousness could therefore lie outside our mental boundaries. It seems highly unlikely that the limits of reality, in its widest sense, must necessarily coincide with the limits of the human mind no matter how far this may be developed and it seems almost certain that, in the recesses of the universe, there must be realities beyond our own, phenomena which our descendants may or may not be able to discern.

Meanwhile 'J'y suis, j'y reste' with all the known evidence indicating that our ideas of reality are rooted in our history going back in an unbroken chain of our ancestors to an 'unconscious' past.

• MASS EXTINCTIONS

It must be borne in mind that since the origin of complex forms of life on earth there have apparently been at least five mass extinctions during which the number of living species collapsed. These extinctions occurred with a periodicity of approximately twenty-six million years and each time these mass extinctions have significantly changed the pattern of life on earth. Each has been followed by rapid recoveries as ecological opportunities were offered to the survivors and humanity was one of the more successful inheritors of the opportunities of the last mass extinction.

The apparently inexorable growth of human population is enveloping and, to a material extent, destroying our habitat and we are beginning to be faced with the question 'What happens next?' The destructive force is now not a transient one as were the earlier ones. In geological terms species do not seem to last all that long - for example vertebrates have had only about two million years. Homo sapiens is relatively young probably not much more than 100,000 years old so that we might reasonably have an 'expectancy' of about 12 million years if cosmological factors only were to be taken into account. We know we have introduced other factors so that 'expectancy' may be shortened and it seems almost certain that sooner or later homo sapiens will disappear, no longer existing here on Earth.

It is possible that some modified form of humanity will have evolved (or been genetically developed?) but this is still in the realms of speculation. What then of 'Values' and of 'Absolutes'?

• THE ORIGIN & FUTURE OF 'VALUES'

May I here recall some of Sherington's ideas which started this trail. In his book 'Man on his Nature' he said:-

"Is `life` a value? ... (Life) is a property with grades of quality and trend... the human mind, co-habiting the planet...if it is to exploit the planet, must in the light of its `values` take the responsibility of judging the grades of sanctity of these other (lives). Is life a 'value'? Surely a means to `value`. This life conflicting with other life even unto death. And there are grades of life (so that) the question would seem to be not whether life is sacred, but how far sacred? (and this leads to a sterner problem). A question which we may think the future of this planet turns upon... whether this planet in its approaching phase is to be the HUMAN PLANET... where all life is to be subservient to... human life. That one life (which) seems to be on its way to something, natural truly, but nevertheless superhuman.

What means shall bring it about? Mind serving 'zest-to-live'? How? By ruthless conquest or beneficent mission? As to which it lies with 'values' to decide... Life taken in general can be no sacred thing. It has enslaved and brutalized the world... If (we) would secure for its community a living welfare on its surface in that aim (we) find ourselves thwarted...by unstemmable fecundity... in blind 'urge-to-live'.

'Addressing then the question 'Is human life sacred?' the reply may well be 'where life has mind, life can suffer'....Human life has among its privileges that of pre-eminence of pain. The civilizations have not rarely ruled that among lives one at least is sacred, namely man's. [Pre-humanity] no life was sacred... For man... partly emancipated... the situation has changed. The rule and the scene are there and are the same apart from himself. The change is in himself. Where have his 'values' come from? (For other forms of life have mind) but not 'values'. 'Wrong' is impossible to them, equally impossible is 'right'...

It is as if the door of Nature has been pushed ajar and man was peeping through, there to get a glimpse of his own story and some fresh understanding of himself. In him evolving mind has got so far as to become critical of its way of life. He feels the curse as well as the blessing attached to the zest-to-live.. Ancient 'values' die hard. We are all often agents of suffering to others. The mill (mankind) has gone through ground out its products in the main by retaining above all the interests of 'self'. The contradiction is that he is slowly drawing from life the inference that altruism, charity, is a duty on thinking life. That an aim of conscious conduct must be the unselfish life but that contradicts all his inherited values... the natural world is wholly uninfluenced by values.. More literally than ever 'there is nothing either good or bad but thinking makes it so' and, outside Man, Nature has in that sense no 'thinking'. He and his 'ethics' stand alone. There is nothing 'good' or 'bad' except himself."

• ABSOLUTES

What then are these 'values'. Given that they must differ in greater or lesser degree for every single person in the world, that it seems we do not and cannot know any Absolutes, where do we go for a guide to what 'values' we should seek to spread throughout the world? What are these 'values' we should endeavour to instill in our children? As has been brought out in various sections of this book almost the only common factor in setting up a system of 'values' for general use is the feature of 'tolerance', the need for each of us to accept we have no means of being sure we are 'right' and others are 'wrong'. We must be tolerant of others' 'values' provided they, in their turn show tolerance, unless their behaviour is such that it becomes so repellent that we feel compelled to intervene physically or mentally.

That evil 'values' exist in one form or another is shown by the behaviour of many people (the abuse and prostitution of children is an outstanding case in point) and there is therefore a valid question - should we permit, or indeed, encourage changes in our Society's laws which would legalize such behaviour in the name of 'tolerance'? Can we stay neutral, and should we remain tolerant, if a Hitler or a Saddam Hussain sets out brutally to enforce their 'values' on the rest of the world? And there are many other problems of a similar, if less dramatic, nature which have to be faced every day.

It is therefore clear that like all the other attempts to determine an Absolute, tolerance is an acceptable and socially desirable 'value' only in certain circumstances. It is easy enough to pay lip service to it as a guiding light but in reality only our own 'values' will determine how far it should be allowed to operate. And this then becomes a circular argument.

• FAIRNESS & DECENCY

In every society and in every culture there will be a type of behaviour stemming from an individual's 'values' which will generally be recognized as 'fair' and 'decent' but this will vary from culture to culture and from group to group. This test - whether a given behaviour will generally be regarded as 'fair' and 'decent'- is a useful guide within that particular culture or group but it loses its effectiveness when cultures or group 'values' clash, as they so often do in our multi-cultural modern world.

Here again the need for tolerance and compromise becomes vital but, in the end, the requirements of the overall group becomes dominant, society while tolerating a certain degree of deviant behaviour must protect its members from being taken over by any group seeking to impose its ideas on the remainder.

• WHAT IS IT ALL FOR?

May I here recall what the sick, six year old boy asked me so many years ago - when he said *'Do you believe in God?'* I could unhesitatingly reply *'Yes'* but when he asked *'Why - What is it all for?'* I was taken aback and had then no answer. Today, after many years of study and discussion, I feel no closer to any satisfying answer to that simple but penetrating question. Therefore I must, I feel, echo Omar Khayyam in saying;-

Myself when young did eagerly frequent
Doctor and Saint, and heard great argument
About it and about: but evermore
Came out by the same door as in I went.

That cannot be the end of the story so, if what I have written should persuade another to attempt to extend, or to confute, my ideas this will provide more than an adequate reward for the time and effort I have put into this attempt at clarifying this fascinating, fundamental and topical subject.

Finally let me end by repeating that old Yorkshire story which, for me at any rate, sums up so well the singularity of our individual 'values', the essential human trait I have tried to explore:-

As the old lady said to her friend:-

Everyone's mad except thee and me; and even thee's a bit queer!

highlighting the uniqueness of everyone's values.

- **The Mandelbrot Picture**

This subject is like a Mandelbrot or Julia picture no matter how much it is investigated each aspect can be elaborated almost without end. I hope this attempt at a broad survey will start a fruitful debate which will enable another writer to provide a more convincing analysis of how 'values' originate and evolve'.

APPENDIX A

Education and the Absorption of 'Values'

There is no known effective way of testing the influence on the way 'values' are modified by education. It is clear this depends very much on the character of the individual student and there can be little doubt the character of the teachers and tutors must also be very important. Indeed for most children this second factor is perhaps the more important in persuading them to 'catch' new 'values' or to modify existing ones.

Some of the principle educational features are considered below:-

- **Forms of Education**

In recent years there has been a good deal of research into the results of different forms of education, into the transmission of knowledge and into the effect of what is taught. This is in place of earlier studies which were largely concerned with why children succeeded in examinations or why they failed. Researchers have been studying the way both teachers and pupils decide on action after they have assessed their social situations. Studies have been made of school 'cultures', strategies and 'negotiations' (especially those between teachers and the taught). Some have concentrated more on 'values' and with 'interactions of values' rather than just with enabling students to absorb sufficient knowledge to pass examinations.

The main questions were:-

- How do teachers and pupils assess school processes, the school personnel and organisation including the lessons, the subjects studied and the attitudes of their peers? What are the main factors which influence them? How do they actually experience their schooling? How do they organise their school activities? What social techniques do they use? How do teachers and students assess their time at school? What form of commitment do they show?

While it is not practicable for me to deal with such questions in detail they are recorded because they are all 'value' questions in one form or another highlighting the central questions - What happens to the interaction of pupils and teachers in schools and how does the educational process help to develop character (change 'values')? This is associated with another important question - How does the educational process help to maintain (or to change) the existing form of society?

Obviously the answers relate to a Western type society for the patterns, and the answers will be very different for other cultures.

- **The New Russia.**

It is worth referring here to the major educational problems currently being faced in the new Russian complex of nations where the basic non-scientific textbooks must be revised because of the fundamental changes taking place in their economic and other 'values'. In Russia itself, and in the nations which they colonised, several generations have been indoctrinated to believe in State Socialism and the common ownership of the means of production. This has collapsed and the Russians are facing many of the evils of Capitalism apparently without reaping much of the material benefits which non-communist nations have enjoyed.

In Russia all the economic text books have to be rewritten largely by people who have little knowledge (and no first-hand experience) of capitalism whether full-bodied or modified. How to describe the way a modern market economy should work without the essential practical knowledge must pose a major problem and it seems very likely that the Russian economy (or economies) will go through some very difficult times before a new balance is reached.

For more than five hundred years Russia has been governed in a strictly dictatorial way and now, in the space of a few years, the whole of the national philosophy is supposed to change. Russians are, it would seem, largely unaccustomed to any kind of dialogue in either economic or social terms. Apparently, at the moment, little works in economic life and there are major problems in social relationships. It seems highly unlikely that any nation can persist for long with this level of uncertainty and social plasticity. The new order needs new 'social values', (new 'myths' perhaps?) to provide suitable and acceptable foundations. What is happening now in their society in general, and in their schools in particular, must have long-lasting consequences.

- **The American Picture**

Studies in America have examined the way their educational system affects the reproduction and continuance of their social class structure. Such studies have led to the general conclusion that there is, in North America at any rate, a high degree of correspondence between school and work so that the present form of their educational system helps to integrate most young people into their current economic system. Overall schools introduce students into the disciplines of the particular type of work required by the economic system by helping to modify their personal 'values' adapting them to the main social 'values' needed in their world of work. This is obviously a very broad statement since there must be a wide variation in the types of 'values' needed in different occupations and at different levels in business and elsewhere. While the fundamental 'values' relating to 'fairness' and 'decency' will remain much the same for all in any particular culture the special 'values' required to be a successful 'pop-star' are likely to be very different from those needed by a doctor, a mathematician or a physicist!

In the schools the interaction of 'values' between administrators and teachers, teachers and students, students and students, and in a way between students and their studies, parallel the hierarchical structure and the division of labour in the outside world. There are somewhat similar vertical lines of authority from administrators to teachers to pupils. Also just as most workers lack control over their work processes so pupils usually lack any real control over their education in terms of the content of their studies although, at a later stage, they usually have a limited set of choices.

Again there is usually a somewhat similar form of motivation by a system of grades and other external rewards, rather than the integration of the student with both the process and the outcome of their studies which would be the natural objective if character formation (modifying 'values') were to be treated as the most important objective. With the more aware students there does come a time, a moment of truth, when they stop working for the approval of teachers or parents and realise they are, in reality, working for themselves. Then the pattern changes and a more mature set of 'values' start to operate. To some extent differences in social relationships within schools reflect the existing social background of the students (and therefore the 'values' they bring with them) as well as their likely future economic position.

- **The Educational System in the United Kingdom**

In the United Kingdom, differentiation between children starts with the way the 'streaming' process works determining how pupils are selected for which schools, and by the early differentiation between State and Public Schools leading to differing opportunities for good university places, or for some other form of further education, or for the essential qualifications for one of the professions.

While the social scale of the parents is an undoubted factor their 'values' are, in many cases even more important. As the earlier quotation from Len Deighton emphasised, character development is in no way the sole prerogative of our schools, whether State or Private. Nor will an Oxbridge exposure necessarily lead to the 'right' values but the university experience will usually provide the opportunity 'to come to terms with life' exposing the individual to wider, and often more stimulating, sets of 'values' shown by the tutors and the other students, both male and female.

While it is not necessarily true for everyone, this exposure to a wider set of 'values' at what may well still be an impressionable age, can help to 'bring out the grain' of the individual character, to reveal any hidden talents and to ensure the individual's 'values' become more firmly established. However I hold strongly that for most students it is important there should be a gap between ending school and moving to a university so that the young man or woman meets the pressures of the real world and gets away from 'the ivory tower' absorbing, or at least being exposed to, the very different 'values' which operate outside the academic circle.

Obviously everyone must go through the experience of 'coming to terms with life' and only a small proportion of students can have the benefit of the university experience. For some it may well prove to be a limiting one imposing, as Len Deighton said, a carapace restricting further development but for most of those who can achieve it, time at a university opens up avenues which may well offer exceptional opportunities for mental development leading to greater maturity.

- **The Class Barrier**

One study in the United Kingdom concentrated on the question 'Why do working class lads get working class jobs?' and the investigation revealed how the 'lads' 'values' led to failure at school thus preparing them for the lower grade manual jobs. In today's conditions this does not necessarily mean they end up in worse paid jobs but for most, not all, their horizons are likely to be more limited.

- **Education for Girls**

There was a parallel study of the differences between the forms of education for girls and for boys which showed a marked difference in the 'values' which the educators sought to communicate. If the importance, particularly in the earliest years of life, of the influence of mothers (and older sisters?) is accepted as an important factor in passing on 'values' to children, from this point of view the education of girls is as important, if not more important, than that of boys. However that seems to be an approach which is far from generally acceptable even in many 'modern' families.

What then is expected of girls and what should they rightly expect from their schooling? It is still true that, in the UK, more boys than girls go to public schools, that more boys go to university and that comparatively few girls specialise in the main scientific subjects in spite of the fact that, from a purely scholastic angle, girls often tend to show better results in tests than do the boys in many areas.

The distinction reflects the generally held view that womens' main function is still to become mothers, to raise children and thus play that major role in instilling the next generation with their initial, and usually most important, 'values'. So that, from this point of view, the present bias in favour of non-scientific subjects in girls' education could perhaps be justified on general terms although at least some girls would undoubtedly benefit from more exposure to the sciences. For in modern conditions numeracy (in the wider sense this would include familiarity with the use of computers) is becoming as important as literacy.

To what extent further education will enable a girl to enjoy life more fully enabling her to gain that vital satisfaction from having and raising children is obviously debatable - it is very much an individual matter. Quite clearly, in some cases, women of an academic cast of mind find the whole business of child bearing and minding limiting and frustrating so that, in their case, additional education, while developing their character in one way, is likely to make them feel even more frustrated if they find they have, by their circumstances, to be 'tied to the kitchen sink' spending the major part of their time with young children. For them the Germanic concept of 'Kinder, Kirke, Kuche' is not a realistic way to zest for life and most therefore find an alternative solution. What this does to their children is another matter.

On the other hand there are many others who, fortunately for our survival, find their greatest satisfaction in their children and in their grandchildren. Nowadays many more manage to combine both types of life spending their early adult years in business, or a profession, then raising a family and often returning to their original occupation when the children are sufficiently grown. In some cases changes in social conditions such as the increased cost of domestic help, and/or the absence of older relatives in the home, tend to make this more difficult than it was.

- **Girls' Education - Further**

There are four important aspects. They are;-

- What are the reasons for educating girls and how do these reasons affect their schooling? Should girls' education differ from that of boys and, if so, in what ways?

Here I would like to refer to a book 'You just don't understand' by Deborah Tannen which deals with the difficulties most men and women experience in communicating with one another. She brings out the way in which differences in early training result in different 'values' in men and women which quite literally make it difficult for the two sexes to communicate clearly and to avoid misunderstanding. She stresses that girls' training tends to encourage 'values' aimed at consensus whereas boys' education helps to develop a competitive spirit. This results later in life in different 'values' which make interaction with the opposite sex, particularly at an intellectual level, that much more difficult. There is therefore a case for a coeducational approach even though it does have certain disadvantages.

In a particular passage she says *"individuals develop patterns of behaviour ('values') based on innumerable influences such as where they grew up, ethnic background, religious or cultural affiliations, class and the vast reservoir of personal experience and genetic inheritance that makes each person's life and personality unique. But seeing a pattern against which to evaluate individual differences provides a starting point to develop not only self-understanding but also flexibility - the freedom to try doing things differently if automatic ways of doing them do not produce entirely successful results".*

For a relatively smooth 'interaction of values' to operate between the two sexes it is helpful to understand gender differences in conversational styles. This may not entirely prevent disagreements from arising but there is a better chance of preventing them spiralling out of control. When sincere attempts to communicate end in stalemate and a beloved partner seems irrational and obstinate, the different languages men and women speak can shake the foundations of our lives. Understanding the other ways of talking is a giant leap across the communication gap between women and men and can provide a major step towards reopening the vital lines of communication.

Reverting now to the main theme of girls' education. The other questions are;-

- What sort of education are girls now receiving in the UK and what effect will this have on their character ('values')?

- What factors affect the interaction of girls with their school life?

- What effects have the changes in State education in Great Britain had on girls' education?

Once again I can only cite these as major areas for consideration and investigation in terms of 'values'- to deal with them in any detail would require more space than I can allow.

• Interactions Between Pupils & Teachers

If the parents have not played their 'proper' part in instilling suitable 'values' what can and should the teachers do to correct what they regard as deficiencies? Clearly in many cases teachers can only provide role models and do but little to tackle the problems of individual children. They, the teachers, can offer, mostly by example, an alternative for children to 'catch', mostly unconsciously, as their own 'values' emerge from their chrysalis. Only in the 'remedial' schools can there be a direct attempt to treat children on a one-to-one basis.

It is common experience that there are some teachers who have a natural gift for creating a sympathetic atmosphere while others, no matter how they try, cannot even maintain control. With some, pupils have an immediate empathy but with others this is completely lacking. It would seem to be largely a matter of the teacher's 'values' stemming not so much from what they say but far more from what they are and do, their 'body language' often speaking far more clearly than their words. The sympathetic teacher will make a dull subject tolerable and an interesting one, exciting. The tone of voice and the accent all play an important part since, if the accent is too strange (and even in some cases incomprehensible), communication must break down and the whole exercise becomes futile.

Most experienced teachers stress the need for discipline and it is an important part of schooling for children to be taught how to adapt themselves to 'rule acceptance' which is a necessary feature of any civilised society. Discipline in schools depends primarily on respect for the teachers as individuals and as a class. Childhood, I suggest, is primarily a time for learning from others and not so much a time for consciously making one's own decisions. Children should therefore be provided with firm leadership, a secure framework, since the great majority need to be led rather than being left to their own devices. The world, particularly the adult world, must still to them be largely incomprehensible so they mostly need clear guidance in choosing from options and deciding on priorities.

Children from warm and sympathetic homes are likely to have acquired the 'values' which provide social skills easing their interaction with both the other children and the teacher. The unlucky ones, those from 'difficult' homes are likely to have acquired 'values' which make it hard for them to fit in. A few will, sadly, be so awkward that they will be assessed as 'maladjusted' and be sent to one of the special schools designed to correct, if they can, some of the 'mistakes' the parent(s) have made.

• **Architecture & Ambience**

The atmosphere and culture of a school is influenced by its architecture, its surroundings and its history. Schools such as Eton, Winchester, Westminster, St. Paul's (or any of the other main Public Schools) attract outstanding masters and pupils often in spite of comparatively limited facilities. The traditions (which strongly influence a school's 'culture') will depend upon the form of its foundation and its history. The way the school is structured and organised (for example whether it is a boarding school or not) also has a major effect. The size of the school will largely determine whether the Head becomes mainly an administrator or whether he plays a more direct part in establishing, and influencing, the 'ethos' of the teaching staff and of the pupils themselves. Often in the larger schools the Head only gets to know a handful of the more senior students (or the more difficult ones!).

In most schools there has been a dramatic change in the shape of the school population, either because of governmental action or from choice, so many more children are staying on to later ages. Originally in most schools there was a fairly flat pyramid with a broad base at the younger ages narrowing down quickly to an apex in the sixth form. Nowadays so many children stay on until sixteen or later that a quite different set of 'interactions' take place. This has special implications particularly in terms of the type of discipline which it is practicable to maintain.

• **Recent Research**

In recent years there have been studies of the elements of school organisation, investigations into teacher and pupil subcultures, and the effect of the actual activities which occur in classrooms (all of which influence the way pupils' 'values' are instilled and modified). The subject is a large one and it is only possible here to indicate some of the main points which are:-

- **What is a school?**

The approach of some writers has been to assume that a school should be treated as a 'client serving' operation organised to socialise the young by modifying existing 'values' (or introducing new ones) enabling them more readily to interact with others and 'fit in' more effectively with the existing social pattern. While this is undoubtedly a part of what schooling aims to do it is far from the full story since the objective should be, as has already been said, to aid the development of the young both physically and mentally so that, as adults, they can fulfil their potential in the home, at work and at leisure in the society in which they live.

One critical writer has said:-

"..there is little consensus... on what their (the schools') primary goal should be. Many ... assume that scholastic achievement (cognitive outcomes) is the primary goal. They measure... effectiveness... by the readily available standardised achievement measures. Others... noting (that) the correlation between academic achievement... and subsequent occupational success is far from perfect, insist that (such a correlation) would be a far better test."

In reality measuring this correlation would be very difficult, if not impossible, and the results would then likely to be so out of date, and general conditions to have changed so much, that the exercise would almost certainly be worthless.

Other writers see the primary objective as the school's ability to influence the students' concept of themselves, that is to instil self-esteem and self-confidence, and to help them to discover their talents. This view fits in well with the study of schooling as an important, a very important, factor in how 'values' are acquired and how they develop.

• Forms of Organisation

In terms of functional organisation there would seem to be three main types of school each of which will have a different effect on the way 'values' are transmitted to the students. The three are the bureaucratic, the 'open system' and the 'total institution' with most schools adopting a mixture of two or more types.

• The Bureaucratic

The Bureaucratic has broadly speaking these characteristics;-

(a) An administrative hierarchy with a structure of command.

(b) Specialised training and a clear career structure for the teaching staff.

(c) Areas of expertise with a division of labour among the expert.

(d) Specific procedures testing how well the bureaucrats fulfil their function.

(e) Formalised and largely impartial rules dealing with the pupils.

COMMENT. All schools need to have some degree of hierarchy, whether explicit or implicit. If the line of authority is not clear, uncertainty is likely to prevail which usually creates an atmosphere of conflict involving strain for the individuals concerned and this may well harm interaction between teachers and pupils. Where a teacher is dealing with a variety of subjects they are likely to be in more continuous touch with the pupils and then 'interaction' is usually far more effective.

- **The Open System**

Here far more weight is given to the relationships between the various parts of the school structure and the social culture in which the school functions. At first sight this should provide a more logical structure since, in crude terms, schools take in raw material (pupils), process them through the classes (teaching and learning) with a product at the end which should be suited to the environment, the society, in which they have to live. However the pupils, the raw material, are far from being standardised units. They all start with very different 'values' and undiscovered talents and the objective must be to help them to evolve as individuals not to produce a set of 'humans' fit only for Sir Thomas More's Utopia.

The main objective should be to help to develop fully functioning individuals who will work constructively to secure their legitimate 'interests', living life with zest while causing the minimum hurt to those they must interact with.

Nor does it seem that this 'Open System' approach gives sufficient weight to such factors as the interaction between teachers (particularly gifted teachers) and pupils which is a powerful and multi-faceted influence something which, for the majority of students, can become the most important influence they experience during their time at school.

It must also be recognised that, during this period, the growing children and young adults are exposed to many other sources of new 'values' such as their contemporaries and the media in its many forms. However the functional approach does have the advantage of focusing attention on the relationship between the School, the culture within which it operates and the educational system itself usually helping students to widen their horizons and to 'take on board' new concepts which can help to modify existing 'values' in a constructive way.

- **Schools as Total Institutions**

For this purpose a 'total' institution can be defined as;-

'A place of residence, or work, where a large number of similarly situated individuals are cut off from their wider society for an appreciable period of time and, together, lead an enclosed formally administered type of life'.

A monastery (even perhaps some British boarding schools?) would seem to go far to meet this definition. The question then is how such a structure stimulating such an education, is likely to affect the acquisition of new 'values' and the modification of existing ones remembering that in real life the proclaimed isolation is far from complete. Even pupils in boarding schools will usually have access to the outside world through radio, television, e-mail, books, magazines and films.

Even in the most structured school there is some degree of autonomy in the way both pupils and teachers interpret the rules which provides scope for different sets of 'values' to develop and to survive. In some of the less 'structured' there is a toleration of 'values' which goes so far as to accept the use of some 'drugs' (which one suspects must lead in some children to sad consequences). It can of course be argued that as, almost inevitably, the pupils will have to meet this problem it could be better for it to be faced earlier rather than later when they, the pupils, are in a position to please themselves. Those basing themselves on conventional wisdom (derived from their experience with alcohol and tobacco) hold that, for most youngsters, it is preferable to delay exposure until at least the age of eighteen, but there are always dangers in making the forbidden into something more tempting particularly for adolescents. And certainly in the Continental countries early exposure to wine does not seem necessarily to have adverse effects.

Obviously pupils at day schools face different problems since they are far more exposed to general community 'values' and are not so segregated from the main stream. The teenager is very powerfully influenced by their peers and if they are at day-school, they are more likely to meet youngsters with a wider spread of 'values' than they would, for much of the time, if they are at boarding school.

This is a debate without end since it lacks hard facts and the answer must, in the end, largely be decided by the character and the 'values' of the individual student when the challenge is met.

- **Text-books**

While within the school most of the 'values' stem from the masters and mistresses there is one factor which normally comes from outside; that is the text-books being used as the framework for studies. While these must, in general, conform with the ethos of the authority financing and controlling the school they normally come from outside reasonably independent sources so they can be a real factor in introducing new ideas and therefore new 'values'.

- **Conclusions**

Schools are, then, often unpredictable organisations where the masters/teachers need to be flexible and creative, willing to react with discretion to changing circumstances, interacting sympathetically with the 'values' of each individual student. (A 'counsel of perfection' which it would be wise not to expect!)

The traditional view of a school as a hierarchical decision-making structure with horizontal divisions into departments and a vertical division into authority levels needs therefore quite extensive modification.

- **What Differences Do Schools Make**

In studies of day school results, quite dramatic variations were found. Thus delinquency rates varied from 4% to 10%, the attendance rate from 77% to 89% and the academic achievement rate (the proportion going on to higher education) from just 8% to 55% going on to further education in one form or another. These results reflect of course not only the effects of the schools themselves but also the material, the types of children, on which the schools 'operated'.

Another interesting analysis indicated that the most effective schools were those where a higher proportion of the pupils were in positions of some authority, where there was a lower level of 'institutional' control, lower rates of physical punishment and where the schools were smaller in size and the pupil/teacher ratios were lower. (Note - the statistics were somewhat suspect because the basic material - the type and quality of the students - did not seem to have been standardised.)

In this particular investigation the concluding summation was relevant. It said:-

"We still need an empirically based theory of schools. Such a theory would depend on the recognition, not just of the uniqueness of the school as a subject for study, but of the deep interconnections by which it coheres, evolves and endures. The school's technologies and structures, rituals and rules can only be appreciated as a complex pattern of interdependencies whose outlines are, at the moment, barely discernible."

This brings out, quite clearly, the need to shift our view of schools from that of academic processors to places for development, both physically and mentally, so that, as adults, the students can fulfil their potential in the home, at work, at leisure and in the society which supports them thus enabling them to live life with the zest.

- **Probabilities, Expectations & 'Values'**

Here it is useful to comment on the way that, usually during the years at school, children begin to take a more reasoned view of the likely consequences of their actions. At home most children are cushioned by their parents, or other supporting adults, against the worst effects of their calculated or uncalculated actions but once the children are at school they often have to face difficulties that their parents may well never be aware of.

At this stage of their development the children have to learn, if they have not already done so at home and at school, to assess (usually subconsciously) the likelihood of being successful in securing their own 'interests' and of balancing off the satisfaction obtained by that particular operation by the possibly adverse and unpleasant results of failure. In other words they start, subconsciously, to assess the 'expectations' involved in any particular action or lack of it. Their perception of the risks involved, and the likely balance, between the satisfaction they will get if they are successful, set against the disappointment, and possible unpleasantness, if they fail will be influenced by their existing 'values' and this process will continue to be used for the rest of their lives.

One thing is certain - motivation is all. What the individual student brings to the school will very largely decide what he or she gets from it. In other words their individual 'values' will determine how they assess the importance, and the value to them, of the scholastic process even though it is highly unlikely they will ever consider their time at school or university in these terms.

- **Summing up**

The scholastic process is, for most in the Western world, a very important part of 'growing up' and the effects on a child of the very different types of environment can hardly be exaggerated since, although many of the basic 'values' will already have been 'caught' in the earliest years from the family, there is no doubt that the changes caused by 'good' schooling, the effect of sympathetic teachers and the new emerging opportunities are all very important factors in future development and, indeed, in one's attitude to life.

Appendix B

Body Language & Interactions

Most people do not know they have a remarkable skill which they use, mostly automatically and subconsciously, to convey information to others particularly of an emotional kind. They start to learn this skill as infants and it is developed throughout their growing years. It is exercised every day they are in communication with other people and it is taken for granted. It is the ability to relate to and to interact with them, to act as social beings and not 'loners'.

To fit into our social world we have to learn how to behave in a socially acceptable fashion. This is obviously largely determined by the culture we were born into and in which we were reared. We do not seem to be born with the instinctive ability to relate to other people and have to learn how to develop both short term and long term relationships which make up much of the substance of living. When the genetically originated sex features develop they may well lead to aggressive behaviour but by then our acquired 'values' will normally provide a restraining influence.

Small babies are notoriously antisocial. They are concerned with survival to the exclusion of all other interests. Somehow this unlikely raw material is transformed over the years into a being whose main objective is, or should be, to live life with zest, to mate and to produce offspring who absorb much the same basic 'values'. The 'monstrous infant' becomes, fortunately in so many cases, the 'caring adult' who finds fulfilment in the joys and pains arising from a wide range of mental and physical relationships.

There are ways, some more effective than others, in starting and developing such relationships particularly in terms of the non-vocal communications which are manifested by all cultures in a greater or lesser degree. When talking, these non-verbal ways of communicating are often more effective than the spoken word not only in conveying information but also, often more importantly, in indicating our personal 'values'. Inappropriate use of body language can cause misunderstanding so that better appreciation of these sometimes subtle manifestations should enable people to appreciate more clearly its significance helping to establish satisfying relationships.

Basically the more formal the setting the more explicit the rules tend to be, ultimately being in a written form. On less formal occasions we have to learn by experience how the unwritten rules should be applied. An obvious example is that of dress - we know it would not be appropriate to go to a funeral dressed as we would for a beach party and it is part of being socially acceptable to learn, and to conform, to the customs of the culture or subculture in which you live.

- **Facial Expressions & Eye Contact**

While the primary function of eyes is to receive information and convey that to the brain they are also important signal transmitters. How people look at us, meet or do not meet, our gaze, how they look away or challenge us with their eyes is all part of the business of conveying information particularly whether they are loving, friendly or the reverse.

Evolution has provided a special signal area in the eyes - the whites - which enable the observer to judge accurately the direction of the gaze for in human interactions it is important to be able to assess quickly whether another person is attending to us or whether their attention is wandering. Looking directly and steadily at another individual's eyes sends so powerful a message that it has to be controlled.

- **Eye Contact Regulates the Flow of Conversation**

Knowing whose turn it is to speak is an important part of any conversation and this is largely governed by the eyes. In some cultures both speak, or shout, together which creates difficulties particularly for any stranger coming from another culture where it is considered polite to let each finish what they are saying. There are some self-centred individuals who never stop talking and in these cases the normal rules cannot apply.

When someone listening wants to speak and indicates this the speaker will sometimes acknowledge they have registered the implied request by a nod or a gesture conveying their need to finish before 'conceding the floor'. So if one is in the position of listening and wanting to make a point it is sensible to keep a watch on the speaker's eyes and when their speech slows down meet their gaze and speak. If necessary breaking into the flow. This lack of eye contact is perhaps one of the reasons why multiple interviews on radio tend to be so chaotic.

- **Group Discussions**

If there is no chairman, eyes can be used to indicate one wishes to speak. In a relaxed atmosphere turn-taking is usually encouraged but if this is not happening then a gesture such as raising a hand or making a gesture may be necessary to call attention to oneself. In speaking it makes sense to stand up so that the maximum eye contact can be established and maintained. Experienced public speakers will know how important it is to vary the sound of their voice to avoid any flatness of tone which inevitably becomes boring.

- **Eyes Reflect Status and Authority**

'Staring a person down' is a common way of asserting authority - if the other person looks away it can be taken as an admission of acceptance. The length of the glance is also important the more senior person making longer glances. On the whole women tend to make more frequent eye contacts than do men reflecting the fact perhaps that, generally, women are more concerned with human relationships.

- **Effects of Personality & Culture**

Most of the people in the Latin Communities, in the Middle East, in Southern Europe and in the races with an African background are brought up in a 'contact' culture where people tend to stand closer when they talk. In the Northern based cultures the conventions are different as is summed up by the criticism of the English that they are 'stand-offish'. This does not mean they are necessarily less sympathetic just that it is necessary to have a code to interpret one set of cultural body language into another

- **Looking, Liking & Trusting**

'Looking' and 'looking back' are usually signs of liking but sometimes not. 'Looking with contempt' is a recognizable feature conveyed as much by bodily motion as by gazing. When the gaze is friendly and is accompanied by a smile the recipient is far more likely to feel friendly since it recognizes them as individuals to which they are far more likely to respond.

This is particularly important when for one reason or another, authority, class, colour, caste or creed one individual is in apparent superiority over another. Robert Burn's "A man's a man for a' that" sums the principle up well. For while men are not equal in all respects, we share a common humanity and if we can find common ground in our 'values' the rest is of comparatively little importance. It is not colour which divides the races but their 'values' flowing from such widely differing cultures.

- **Pupil Signals**

When emotions are stirred up the pupils tend to dilate conveying a message of liking or disliking. Returning a 'wide-eyed' glance signals either liking or dislike. While staring with dilated pupils is usually a sign of intense liking or 'spoiling for a fight'. The rest of the body language will indicate which!

- **Reading Facial Expressions**

Often a person's facial expression is a better guide to their real feelings than their words. Some seem inscrutable and the Eastern races have been noted for this partly because they were trained to 'keep their countenance' in business matters and partly because Westerners were not skilled in reading the signs.

We rely on facial expressions very considerably to interpret another person's intentions, to assess their likely 'values' and to help in passing information about our own to them. However it must be remembered that dissimulation is something learned early in life and not everyone has 'an open countenance'!

It is worth recording that when Darwin became interested in this subject he sent a questionnaire with sixteen points to various parts of the world to see to what extent facial and bodily gestures showed similarities for very different cultures and recorded that 'the same state of mind is expressed throughout the world with remarkable uniformity although there were inevitably differences'

Studies of infants show they respond more readily to face-shaped objects, they smile at faces and react to eyes so that a pair of eye-like dots can readily call forth a smile.

- **The Language of Touch**

Touches from people such as doctors, nurses, the hairdresser carry no emotional or personal implications but apart from those, touching is often a more powerful means of communication than words. How we touch and allow ourselves to be touched is highly significant of our personal relationships.

Socially we have very specific rules as to the parts of the body which it is proper to touch and the circumstances in which touching is allowed or encouraged, the most obvious being the lovers need to be able to touch at all times.

Touching also indicates how 'power' is distributed among individuals and the way intimates, friends, acquaintances and strangers are susceptible to touching is ruled by conventions which differ from one culture to another.

Sometimes it is polite to touch - the handshake (which, originally, was apparently used to show there was no concealed weapon) is common to many cultures and kissing in one form or another is equally so. On the whole there is more touching among women than men perhaps because, in some cultures, there can be partly sexual overtones which men prefer to avoid.

- **Greeting and Parting**

An easy greeting will make most meetings run more smoothly and the right kind of 'Goodbye' will make an impression likely to carry over to the next meeting. To understand and properly to interpret both will enable one to respond in the most suitable fashion.

Lowering the body or bowing the head are universal signs acknowledging superiority and judging by the behaviour of chimpanzees may well be innate.

- **Conclusion**

This again is a subject which can only be touched upon - it should probably be part of our general education because the implications are so little understood. Certainly it is part and parcel of the way humanity conveys information about its 'values' and 'interests' sometimes more effectively than by the spoken word.

INDEX

A
aborigines VI, 146
abortion   48
absolutes   XII-XIII, 5, 42-3, 64, 115, 117, 121, 124, 155
action chain 86-8
Acton, Lord 109
Adkins, W.H. 120
Adler, Alfred 94
adolescense 35-7
adulthood 37-9
aging 45-8
American education 161-3
Ancient Egypt VII
Ancient Greece 118
anthropology V
antiphon 64
Aquinas, Thomas 64-5
architecture and ambience in schools 170
Aristotle 64, 123-6
Aspergers Syndrome X, 60

B
behaviour 82-3, 100-1
behaviourism 129-138
Berlin, Isaiah XIII
Bible, Genesis I
biology and the law 70
body language and behaviour 138, 180
    eye contact 181-3
    facial expression 181, 184
    greetings & partings 186
    group discussions 182
    personality & culture 183
    pupil signals 183
    touch 185
bonding 75-7
Book Of The Dead VIII, 118
Bradley, General Omar 139
brain, research 58
Buddhism XIII, 8, 94

C
character, human formation of 106
children 29-33
children, disturbed, education of 104
Christianity XIV, 4-5, 8, 51, 54, 92, 141, 144
class barriers 164
colonialism 109
commandments, ten XIII, 48, 80, 118
Communism 17, 108
conscience 50-2
consciousness & death 151
cosmologies 147
crises, middle aged 43
cruelty 33
Crusoe, Robinson 6
culture, western 15-8
curve, the normal 59

D
Darwin, Charles XI, 53-6, 140
Dawkins, Richard 149
death 151

Deighton, Len 40-1
demons 59
development, early 143-5

E
Eaves, Eysenck, Martin 21, 26
education 40, 94-112, 159-179
    religous 96
    organisation 172
    theory of 97, 100
    and values 105
    absorbtion of values 159
    forms of 159
    recent research 170
Ehrlich 65
Einstein XI
eskimos VI
ethics and values I, 113-128
ethnological perspective 61
ethology 65-70
euthanasia 48
evil 142
extinctions, mass 152

F
fairness & decency 156, 100
factors, basic 19
family relationships and the law 44
Fox 61
Frazer, Sir James 8
Freud XI, 32, 97

G
genetic inheritance 3, 22, 69, 88-90

Gifford lectures 2-4
girls, education 164-8
God, the nature of 113
Golden Bough, The 8, 75
good, the meaning of 115-121
group order & fairness 78-80
Gruter, Dr Margaret 24, 55, 61

H
Hinduism XIII, 84, 90, 94, 118
Homer 120-1
humanities 94
Hume, David 113
Huxley 54

I
incest 88
Indian Civil Service 107
indoctrination 29
insemination, artificial 88
interaction, between pupils & teachers 168
Islam 17
Ivory Tower 40

J
James, William XIII, XIV, 1, 10
Judaism VIII, XIII, 33, 64, 80, 92
justice & fairness 58, 121

K
Kant 115, 121
Khayyam, Omar 156
kin selection 72-5

L

law, biological studies & the 70
evolution of 61-5
family 77-8
living 67
natural 64-5
role of 81-2
language 150-1
Lawrence, D.H. 125-6
life - a boon? 48
Locke 115

M

MacDonald, John D 142-3
Malthus 55
marriage 41-2, 84-6, 91-2
Martineau, Harriet 54
middle age 43-4
Miller, Dr Alice 33-4
Mills 115
miracles 13-4
mind - structure of 135
Moore, G.E. Principia Ethica 115, 127
morals 126, 114
mother-infant bonding 75
Muslims 84
myths I, VII, 9, 17, 54, 121, 147-150

N

nature & nurture 19-52
Neanderthal man 150-1

O

objectives 12

order - group 78-80
Orwell, George 89

P

pair bonding 84-6
Paul St. 5, 16
personality 20-1, 136-7
perspectives - historic 146-7
philosophy & values 135
ethics & religion XIV
individual 101
physiology - factors 132-3, 146
Piaget 98-9
Plato 119, 123-4
pragmatism XII, 10
probabilites & truth 134
procreation 90-1

R

reasoning 135-6
relativity XI
religion & beliefs 7, 147-150
rights & responsibilities 83
Roman Empire 18
Roosevelt, Franklin 50
rules - making & obeying 57-8
Russia - education in 160-1

S

saints & demons 59-60
Schiller XIII
schools 171
scientific method V, X, 102-4, 110, 146
scientific revolution 146
Sermon - on the Mount 141

sexuality 83-4, 93
sexual equality 93
Shakespeare 19, 142
Shaw, Bernard XVIII
Sherrington, Sir Charles 2-4, 21
social attitudes 28
Socrates 122-4
sophism 120, 122
Spencer, Herbert 94

T
Tannen, Deborah 166
text books 175
Thales 64
Thucidides 122
tolerance & its limits 60
Tolstoy 125
touch, the language of - see
    'body language'

U
United Kingdom, education in
    163-4
universe IV, VIII, 12
U.S.A. XIV, 16, 161

V
value judgements III, IV, 5,
values,
    biological origin 24-6
    changes in 10-11, 22-3
    educational 105
    future of 15, 153-5
    interaction of 145
violence 33

W
will, free 125
Wittengstein 6
Wordsworth 53
work 39

Bibliography

Acton, Lord - *Historical Essays and Studies*
Adkins, W. H. -
Aquinas, Thomas -
Aristotle - *Metaphisics*
Armstrong, Karen - *Muhammed*
Berlin, Isaiah
Bible - *Genesis 2:7.*
       Exodus 3:14
Birtchnell, John - *How Humans Relate*
Book of the Dead - *British Museum Dictionary of Ancient Egypt*
Bronowski, J - *The Ascent of Man*
Bruner, Jerome - *Acts of Meaning*
       Actual Minds Possible Worlds
       On Knowing
       Toward a Theory of Instruction
Clark, Kenneth - *Civilisation*
Clough, Arthur Hugh - *Advice to a doctor on treatment*
Darwin, Charles - *The Descent of Man*
       The Origin of Species
Dawkins, Richard - *River out of Eden*
Deighton, Len - *Sinker*
Descartes, Rene - *Cogito*

Eaves, Eysenck &n Martin - *Genes, Culture and Personality*
Ehrlich
Frazer, Sir James - *The Golden Bough*
Freud, Sigmund - *Civilization and its Discontents*
Gregory, Richard L. - *The Oxford Companion to the Mind*
Gruter, Dr Margaret - *Law and the Mind*
Hegel, G. W. F. - *The Philosophy of Right*
Hodgson, David - *The Mind Matters*
Honderich, Ted - *The Oxford Companion to Philosophy*
Hume, David - *Discourses concerning Natural Religion*
Huxley, T. H. - *The Coming of Age of The Origin of Species*
James, William - *Pragmatism*
     The Meaning of Truth
Jones, Steve - *In the Blood*
Khayyam, Omar - *The Rubyat*
Kierkegaard, Soren -
Lawrence, D. H. - *Cypresses*
Locke, John - *Essay concerning Human Nature*
Macdonald, John D. - *A Tan and Sandy Silence*
MacIntyre, Alisdair - *A Short History of Ethics*
Magee, Bryan - *The Great Philosophers*
Malthus T. R, - *On Population*
Martineau, Harriet
Mason, Phillip - *The Men who ruled India*
Miller, Dr Alice - *The Drama of being a Child*
Moore, G. E. - *Principia Ethica*
Morris, Desmond - *The Naked Ape*
Nietzshe, Friedrich W. - *Thus spoke Zarathustra*
Orwell, George - *1984*
Piaget

Bibliography

Plato - *Apology, Phaedras, Republic Theaetetus*
Roberts, J.M. - *History of the World*
Romer, John - *Testament (The Bible and History)*
Rose, Steven - *The Making of Memory*
Russell, Bertrand - *History of Western Philosophy*
Satre, Jean Paul - *Being & Nothingness*
Schiller
Shakespeare - *Hamlet*
Shaw, Bernard - *Reason*
Sherrington, Sir Charles - *Gifford Lectures 1937-8*
                          Man on his Nature
Smart, Ninian - *The World's Religions*
Spencer, Herbert - *Education*
Spinoza, Baruch - *Ethics*
Tannen, Deborah - *You Just Don't Understand*
Tarnas, Richard - *The Passion of the Western Mind*
Tolstoy, Leo - *Memoirs of a Madman*
Wittgenstein, Ludwig - *On Certainty*
                       Philosophical Investigations
Wordsworth, William - *A Poet*